I0409305

DISRUPTING THREAT FINANCES

Using Financial Informationto Disrupt Terrorist Organizations

Wesley J. L. Anderson

Joint Special Operations University (JSOU) Report 08-3

The Joint Special Operations University Press

Hurlburt Field, Florida 2008

On the cover: Automatic weapons along with dozens of rocket propelled grenades (RPGs), hand grenades, and ammunition found during a security operation conducted by coalition security forces in Afghanistan. (DoD photo)

Comments about this publication are invited and should be forwarded to Director, Strategic Studies Department, Joint Special Operations University, 357 Tully Street, Alison Building, Hurlburt Field, Florida 32544. Copies of this publication may be obtained by calling JSOU at 850-884-1569; FAX 850-884-3917.

This work was cleared for public release; distribution is unlimited.

The views expressed in this publication are entirely those of the author and do not necessarily reflect the views, policy or position of the U.S. Government, Department of Defense, United States Special Operations Command, or the Joint Special Operations University.

Table of Contents

FOREWORD

Terrorist financing is a critical issue in the current fight against transnational terrorist networks or groups. Conceptually, this issue is considered one of numerous types of terrorist support activities; however, as the author argues quite persuasively, it may be the most important of these activities. Major Wesley Anderson initially developed the concept for this paper while a student at the Army Command and General Staff College and with the School for Advanced Military Studies (SAMS) at Fort Leavenworth, Kansas. SAMS published an original version of this monograph electronically in April 2007. Joint Special Operations University (JSOU) asked the author to adapt his work to JSOU's monograph requirements for adding to its series of works on terrorist networks and their support structures.

Major Anderson provides an excellent overview of terrorist financing and expands upon how it fits into the broader construct of threat financing. He articulates the significant challenges any government faces in trying to interrupt the terrorist networks use of the global financial system. The sheer immensity of this system provides ample opportunity for terrorists to operate undetected or unhindered. He also highlights that the very international nature of the global economic system presents enormous challenges in trying to coordinate amongst the almost 200 sovereign states that comprise the current world order.

In addition, each of these nations face an internal challenge similar to that facing the U.S., how do the individual country's internal security, legal, and financial governmental organizations work together to meet the significant threat that terrorist networks pose to national sovereignty. In the U.S., we describe this situation as the interagency process, but it is a challenge facing any bureaucracy, and all governments are a bureaucracy in some fashion. As one reads this monograph, many of Major Anderson's recommended solutions hinge upon the requirement for significant overhaul in the U.S. national security system and, by implication, systems in many of the world's countries.

The reader will find the appendices quite informative. Major Anderson compiled an exhaustive survey of terrorist financing mechanisms, U.S. authorities and legal statutes, and a listing of both U.S. and international organizations involved in combating terrorist financing. These appendices, combined with his insightful analysis of the current antiterrorist financing campaign and potential improvement areas, provide a superb overview and summary for someone new to the fight or an excellent reference tool for those already waging it. Readers can obtain the author's original work, released for public use, at the Defense Technical Information Center's Public Scientific and Technical Information Network (http://stinet.dtic.mil). - Michael C. McMahon, Lt Col, USAF Director, JSOU Strategic Studies Department

ABOUT THE AUTHOR

Major Wesley Anderson began his Army service in 1988 an enlisted medic in the Army Reserves. In 1993, he was commissioned as a Distinguished Military Graduate from the Creighton University ROTC Program and served as a medical-surgical nurse and critical care nurse at Fitzsimons Army Medical Center, Aurora, Colorado and the Institute of Surgical Research, Brooke Army Medical Center, San Antonio, Texas.

After completing his Special Forces training in 2000, Captain Anderson was assigned to the 10th Special Forces Group Airborne SFG (A), Fort Carson, Colorado. As detachment commander for Operational Detachment Alpha 045, he was tasked to Bosnia as the J3 for the Combined Joint Special Operations Task Force for Operation Joint Forge, and he deployed with ODA 045 in conjunction with A Company, 10th SFG (A) to Kosovo for Operation Joint Endeavor. As commander for Headquarters and Headquarters Company (HHC), Captain Anderson deployed the company in support of Operation Iraqi Freedom (OIF I).

Major Anderson's following assignment was as a current operations officer, Special Operations Division and as a defense planner for the Bi-National Planning Group, U.S. Northern Command, Peterson AFB, Colorado. He is currently assigned to the Surgical Trauma Intensive Care Unit, as the head nurse, at Brooke Army Medical Center, San Antonio, Texas.

Major Anderson holds a Bachelors of Science Degree in Nursing from Creighton University, an Executive Masters Degree in Business Administration from Benedictine College, and a Masters Degree in Military Arts and Sciences from the Command and General Staff College. He is a graduate of the United States Army Medical Basic Officer Course, Infantry Officer's Advanced Course, Special Operations Qualification Course, Command and General Staff Officer Course, Advanced Operators Warfighters Course, and the Advanced Military Studies Program.

ACKNOWLEDGMENTS

I would like to thank all the individuals and organizations that assisted me in completing this work. Without everyone's time and energy this monograph would never have been accomplished.

In addition, I would like to offer my gratitude to Simone Ledeen, Christopher Burdick, Lieutenant Colonel Charles Vance (Retired) and Dr. James Schneider for going above and beyond with their help, insight, and patience with regard to this project. Finally, I would like to thank my wife and children for their support and understanding during this endeavor.

De Oppresso Liber

Major Wesley J.L. Anderson, U.S. Army

INTRODUCTION

There are two things a brother must always have for jihad, himself and money. *Al Qaeda Operative[1]*

This work investigates whether or not the disruption of terrorist financing as part of an integrated and holistic approach is an effective way to enhance United States (U.S.) security, disrupt terrorist operations, and mitigate terrorist effects on U.S. strategic interests. Too often, individuals around the world talk about winning the war on terrorism and defeating terrorist organizations, such as Al Qaeda; however, as long as there are intolerant and violent humans on this earth, terrorism will not be defeated. Unfortunately, terrorism, prostitution, and drugs are criminal ventures with long histories, and they will probably always be present.[2]

The focus of counterterrorism efforts, therefore, should not be on the elusive goal of "defeating terrorism," but instead should be on understanding the underlying grievances, organizational structure, and vulnerabilities associated with terrorist organizations and networks.[3] Once the U.S. gains these understandings, it should focus on disrupting terrorist organizations and making it more dangerous and costly for them to conduct their operational, logistical and financial activities.

Since the terror attacks of 11 September 2001, detecting and preventing terrorist activities have been top priorities for the United States Government (USG).[4] One of the goals of President George W. Bush's Global War on Terrorism (GWOT) is to deny terrorist groups access to the international financial system, to impair their ability to raise funds, and to expose, isolate, and incapacitate their financial networks.[5] Like most organizations, terrorist groups need financing to organize, recruit, train, and equip adherents.[6] If the U.S. is going to be effective in its fight against terrorist organizations, however, it must expand President Bush's financial dimension of the fight beyond the role of trying to deny terrorist access to financing and progress into the realm of using financial information as the "string" that leads to all aspects of terrorist operations. By disrupting access to financial resources and, more importantly, following its trail, the USG, through coordinated intelligence, investigations, prosecutions, sanctions, and diplomacy within the Interagency (IA) community, private sector, allies, and partner nations, can enhance U.S. security, disrupt terrorist operations, and mitigate terrorist effects on U.S. strategic interests.

Although extensive information has been published on the subject of terrorist financing, the author believes that the Department of Defense (DoD) current contributions to this effort fall short in the areas of IA facilitation and integration along with the advancement of nonkinetic options outside the realm of classified plans and congressional testimony. The author attributes DoD's lack of rigor on the subject of terrorist financing to four factors:

a. The disruption of terrorist financing is seen as a nontraditional role (nonkinetic option).

b. No policy statement has been developed.

c. No way ahead has been developed.

d. The DoD has no defined authorities under U.S. law and regulations with regard to threat financing nor does DoD have an overarching directive.

Without extensive IA facilitation and integration and advancement of all viable options to disrupt terrorist organizations, DoD is not fully leveraging its massive capabilities and resources.

This work examines the hypothesis that the effects of terrorist organizations on U.S. strategic interests can be disrupted and mitigated through:

a. Giving an existing organization the mandate and funding authority to coordinate and direct the actions of all USG agencies (without stifling their flexibility or resources) against terrorist organizations.

b. Enhancing multilateral cooperation and information sharing with IA, private sector, allies, and partner nations.

c. Utilizing commercial off the shelf (COTS) technology to create an integrated communication network between the IAs, private sector, allies, and partner nations.

d. Establishing a DoD policy and way ahead.

BACKGROUND

This morning, a major thrust of our war on terrorism began with the stroke of a pen. Today, we have launched a strike on the financial foundation of the global terror network...we will direct every resource at our command to win the war against terrorists: every means of diplomacy, every tool of intelligence, every instrument of law enforcement, every financial influence. We will starve the terrorists of funding, turn them against each other, rout them out of their safe hiding places and bring them to justice. - *President George W. Bush, 24 September 2001[7]*

Terrorist States, Organizations, Networks, and Individuals

As used in this monograph, the term *terrorist state* includes the five countries currently designated as State Sponsors of Terror by the Secretary of State pursuant to three laws, the term *terrorist organization* includes the 42 organizations currently designated as Foreign Terrorist Organizations (FTOs) by the Secretary of State, and the term *terrorist* includes the 426 individuals and organizations designated as Specially Designated Global Terrorists (SDGTs).[8] In addition, *terrorist* includes any person or organization that intends to carry out or aid, assist, or support an act of domestic or foreign terrorism as those terms are defined by Title 18 United States Code (USC), sections 2331(1) and (5).

The FTOs (shown in Appendix A) confronting the U.S. are nonmonolithic, transnational movements of extremist organizations, networks, and individuals, and their state and nonstate supporters. For example, Al Qaeda currently functions as the terrorist movement's vanguard and remains, along with its affiliate groups and those inspired by them, the most dangerous present manifestation of the enemy. What unites the Al Qaeda movement is a common vision and set of ideas about the nature and destiny of the Islamic world. These terrorists are fueled by a radical ideology. They seek to expel Western power and influence from the Muslim world and establish regimes that rule according to a violent and intolerant distortion of the Islamic faith.[9]

Terrorist Financing

For the purposes of this monograph, the term *terrorist financing* is defined as any form of financial support of terrorism or financial support of those who encourage, plan, or engage in terrorism. The term *fund* refers to financial holdings, cash accounts, securities, and debt obligations.[10]

The sources, movement, and storage of the various alternative financing mechanisms used by terrorist organizations (see Appendix B) to finance their networks are as diverse as the many different cultures of the world. Some terrorist organizations such as those in Europe, East Asia, and Latin America rely on common criminal activities such as extortion, kidnapping, narcotics trafficking, counterfeiting, and fraud to support their operations. Other terrorist organizations, such as those in the Middle East, tend to rely on not-for-profit organizations, donations from individuals and businesses (both witting and unwitting), and funds skimmed from charitable organizations. Still other terrorist organizations rely on State Sponsors of Terror, although this method of funding appears to be decreasing in recent years.[11]

Regardless of the method terrorist organizations use to fund their operations, two facts should be remembered:

a. Terrorists, like all criminals, focus on crimes of opportunity in vulnerable locations throughout the world.

b. Terrorists will continue to adapt and create new methods of financing their organizations in order to avoid detection and maintain a viable financial infrastructure to facilitate their end state.[12]

Efforts to determine the scope of the problem with regard to terrorist financing meet with two primary difficulties:

a. The USG has not determined with any precision how much money terrorist organizations such as Al Qaeda raise, or from whom, or how they spend their money.

b. Most of the Al Qaeda and other Islamist terrorist groups funding originates and is disbursed outside the U.S. and its jurisdiction.[13]

Based on the extrapolation of current data available, however, terrorist organizations are experiencing minor difficulties in raising funds for their organizations and operations. For example, the Central Intelligence Agency (CIA) estimates that it cost Al Qaeda, which was the major sponsor of the Taliban in Afghanistan, about $30 million per year to sustain its operations before 9/11, an amount raised almost entirely through donations. In 2001, The U.S. seized $264,935,075 in assets belonging to the Taliban that were under U.S. jurisdiction.[14] These numbers show that Al Qaeda had eight years, nine and one half months worth of operating expenses under the jurisdiction of one country in support of one organization. Although the U.S., its allies, and partner nations have made significant strides since 9/11, it is premature to assume that terrorist organizations are having difficulty funding their organizations and operations. What is important is that the global effort against terrorist financing has made it more expensive and more difficult to raise and move funds.

Like other criminal organizations, terrorist organizations such as Al Qaeda adapt quickly and effectively, creating new challenges with respect to understanding their financing mechanisms. However, unlike the pre-9/11 Al Qaeda model of a single organization raising money that is then funneled through a central source (finance committee), the U.S. is now contending with an array of loosely affiliated groups, each raising funds on its own initiative.[15]

Financial facilitators are at the core of terrorist organizations' revenue stream. Although there is little question that the arrests and deaths of several important facilitators have decreased the funds terrorist organizations have at their disposal, they still have the ability to fund their operations. Based on the moderate success against financial facilitators, terrorist organizations are beginning to rely more on the physical movement of money and other informal methods of value transfer, which can pose significant challenges for those attempting to detect and disrupt terrorist financing.[16] Because of the complexity and variety of ways to collect and move small amounts of money in a vast worldwide financial system, gathering intelligence on terrorist organizations financial flows will remain an elusive target for the foreseeable future.[17]

Terrorist organizations appear to be migrating toward a) alternative financing mechanisms such as cash couriers, alternative remittance systems, stored value cards, digital currency, and Islamic banking; b) not-for-profit organizations, including front organizations and charities; and c) criminal activity, including trade and commodities based schemes and benefits fraud.[18] It is important to remember, however, that although there appears to be a current trend toward certain methods of moving funds, terrorists still use other less favorable or even unknown methods to support their organizations.[19]

Importance of Terrorist Finances

Actual terrorist operations require only comparatively modest funding.[20] Louise Richardson, Executive Dean of Radcliff Institute of Advanced Studies, argues "that terrorist organizations can exist on very little funding ... because their most important resource is that they have an ideology that is able to win them recruits. They have an argument that they're making successfully about depicting us [U.S.] as their enemy. And we're letting them make that argument." [21]

However, international terrorist groups need significant amounts of money to organize, recruit, train, and equip new adherents and to otherwise support their infrastructure.[22] Terrorist organizations must have financing to pay for protection (such as safe havens), to bribe corrupt public officials, for recruiting, for indoctrination and training, for general operational expenses and equipment, to provide logistical support, to communicate, to increase their organizations infrastructure, to support operatives' families, to provide support to families of martyrs, to fund humanitarian efforts, and for various other sundry items.[23] In short, terrorist organizations require considerable amounts of funds to be raised, moved, and stored through various means to conduct operations. These funds leave identifiable and traceable footprints in the global financial systems, and these footprints must be pursued both downstream, to identify future perpetrators and facilitators, and upstream, to identify funding sources and disrupt supporting entities and individuals.[24]

The DoD Dictionary of Military and Associated Terms defines a *decisive point* as "a geographic place, specific key event, critical factor, or function that, when acted upon, allows commanders to gain a marked advantage over an adversary or contribute materially to achieving success."[25] Based on the fact that terrorist organizations require financing to operate, finances are a critical factor, and disrupting finances will contribute to the U.S., its allies, and partner nations' success in the fight against terrorism.

After the 9/11 attacks, the U.S. and its allies quickly recognized the urgent need to detect, dismantle, and deter terrorist financing networks around the world.[26] The 9/11 attacks could never have been executed without the logistical assistance of a sophisticated and well entrenched support network. The *9/11 Commission Report* demonstrates that the 19 hijackers were funded and facilitated by dozens of individuals, cells, front organizations, and affiliates that provided essential logistical support. Long term logistical planning also went into the earlier bombings of the United States Ship (USS) *Cole* and the embassies in East Africa. Accordingly, an individual, group, or state that provides funds, travel documents, training, or other support for terrorist activity is no less important to a terrorist network than the operative who executes the attack. A key lesson learned from 9/11 is that counterterrorism efforts must target financial and logistical cells with the same vigor as operational cells.[27]

The DoD Dictionary of Military and Associated Terms defines a *node* as "an element of a system that represents a person, place, or physical thing."[28] A close examination of terrorist networks reveals there are key nodes in their organizations that have become the preferred conduits used by terrorists to fund and facilitate attacks.[29] If, therefore, the world is serious about disrupting the terrorists' operating environment, countries need to look at key nodes in the network, such as financing, which terrorist's organizations use to raise, launder, and transfer funds.[30]

One of the advantages of focusing on financial nodes is that many of them are not peculiar to one terrorist group. For example, the International Islamic Relief Organization (IIRO) finances the activities of a diverse cross section of international terrorist groups. From 1986 to 1994, Osama bin Laden's brother-in-law, Muhammad Jamal Khalifa (killed in 2007), headed the IIRO's Philippines office, through which he channeled funds to Al Qaeda affiliates, including Abu Sayyaf and the Moro Islamic Liberation Front (MILF). In 1999, an IIRO employee in Canada was linked to the Egyptian Islamic Jihad. More recently, official Palestinian documents seized by Israeli forces in April 2002 established that the IIRO donated at least $280,000 to Palestinian charities and organizations that U.S. authorities have linked to Hamas.[31]

By redirecting additional assets toward financial intelligence to enhance the monitoring of funds through the financial nodes of various terrorist networks, the U.S., its allies, and partner nations can increase the amount of actionable intelligence for the consumer, which will further assist in the disruption of terrorist operatives, sympathizers, financiers, and future actions.[32] However, attempting to understand and monitor terrorist financial nodes to garner actionable intelligence is hindered by several ongoing challenges, such as:

a. Speed, diversity, and complexity of the means and methods terrorists use for raising and moving funds

b. Commingling of terrorist money with legitimate funds

c. Many layers and transfers between donors and the ultimate recipients of the funds

d. Existence of unwitting participants

e. Lack of a clearly defined and integrated chain of authority and oversight within the U.S.

f. Lack of a common communications architecture, familiarity with the information, and process for sharing within and between the U.S., its allies, and partner nations.[33]

Although financial information can create actionable intelligence by establishing a solid and reliable link between individuals, networks, and organizations, taking disruptive action is not always the most desirable course of action.[34] Rather than starve terrorists of funding, as was the approach early in the fight against terrorists, the current intelligence community approach appropriately focuses on using financial transactions, in close coordination with other types of intelligence, to identify and track terrorist groups.[35] By using these passive and synergistic intelligence techniques, countries improve their analyses of how terrorist organizations raise, move, and utilize their financial assets and develop a better understanding of their overall organizational structure, in addition to their interrelationship with other organizations and networks.

Economic Strategies and Efforts Against Terrorist Financing

Since 1995, the USG has used economic sanctions as a tool against international terrorist organizations, which was a significant departure from the traditional use of sanctions against countries or regimes. The scope of U.S. sanctions against terrorist organizations significantly expanded immediately following the events of 9/11 when President Bush issued Executive Order (EO) 13224.[36] President Bush's combination of EO 13224 and other programs targeting terrorist organizations and governments that support terrorists constituted a wide ranging assault on international terrorism, its supporters, and financiers.[37]

The U.S. strategy against terrorist financing has evolved considerably since the early days of EO 13224. While diminishing terrorist funds remains the most visible aspect of the U.S. approach, it is no longer the only, or even most important, aspect.[38] USG efforts to combat terrorist financing both at home and abroad include a number of interdependent activities:

a. Terrorist designation. First, the USG designates terrorists and then blocks or passively monitors their assets and financial transactions, and supports the similar efforts of other countries in this regard. In addition, the United Nations generally designates those same terrorist organizations internationally under such United Nations Security Council Resolutions (UNSCRs) as 1267, 1373, and 1617 in an attempt to isolate them from the global financial network.

b. Intelligence and law enforcement. Second, U.S. intelligence and law enforcement personnel conduct operations and investigations, and exchange information and evidence with each other and their respective counterparts abroad.

c. Setting international standards. Third, U.S. agencies work through international entities, such as the United Nations and the intergovernmental Financial Action Task Force (FATF), to help facilitate international standards which assist in disrupting terrorist financial nodes (see Appendix E).

d. International training and technical assistance programs. Finally, the USG provides training and technical assistance directly to vulnerable countries and works with its allies and partner nations to leverage resources to facilitate these efforts.[39]

Since terrorist organizations often operate internationally, a key component of the fight against terrorists is to build effective and integrated international cooperation. Diplomacy is one of the critical aspects for winning the political commitment from which cooperation in other areas originates, and the U.S. State Department (DoS), through its embassy teams, plays a vital role in that effort (see Appendix D). Through enhanced cooperation and complete integration with intelligence activities, law enforcement officials will develop a better understanding of the situation and ultimately enhance the U.S. disruption of terrorist organizations.[40] Through active integration and cooperation that entails a clearly defined chain of authority and oversight, a shared communications architecture, and enhanced utilization of resources, the U.S., its allies, and partner nations will be successful in detecting, disrupting, and dismantling terrorist financial networks throughout the world.

Effects of U.S. and International Efforts Against Terrorist Financing

The U.S. and the international community have achieved successes in disrupting the financial underpinnings of terrorist networks. Raising and moving funds are now harder, costlier, and riskier for terrorist organizations. The U.S., its allies, and partner nations have frozen and seized terrorist assets; exposed, monitored, and dismantled known channels of funding when warranted; deterred donors; arrested key facilitators; and built higher hurdles in the international financial system to prevent abuse by terrorists' organizations.[41]

As of 31 December 2005, according to the U.S. Treasury Department Terrorist Asset Report, the total value of blocked assets totaled $13,793,102.[42] In addition, more than $471 million in assets relating to five designated State Sponsors of Terrorism is located within U.S. jurisdiction. Of that amount, $368 million was blocked pursuant to economic sanctions imposed by the U.S. and administered by the Office of Foreign Assets Control (OFAC). The remaining balance of $102,600,000 in assets represents nonblocked funds of individuals and entities from Iran and Syria.[43]

The amount of assets blocked under the public designation process is not, however, a primary measure of effectiveness of antiterrorism programs. Countries that have been declared as supporters of terrorist activities whose assets are not currently blocked by a sanctions program are extremely reluctant to hold assets in the U.S.[44] In addition, the blocking of terrorist organizations' assets, with the notable exception of the Taliban, tends to be a small amount of funds.

The usefulness of public designation process lies in four results that are less direct than the amount of assets blocked in the U.S. Public designation:

a. Encourages other countries to take their own actions against suspected terrorist financing networks.

b. Discourages less ardent supporters from wittingly funding terrorist organizations for fear of being designated a terrorist and having their bank accounts frozen.

c. Facilitates the dismantling of entire terrorist financial networks, making it more difficult for terrorist organizations to raise funds and finance terrorist operations

d. Causes terrorists to resort to other nontraditional, more costly and uncertain, but still serviceable mechanisms for moving assets globally.[45]

While freezing the funds of terrorists can be used as a tool against terrorist organizations, it is by no means the only or most effective means to disrupt these organizations.

MECHANICS OF TERRORIST FINANCING

> For more than 2,000 years, military strategists have recognized the truism that armed conflict cannot be waged until it has been financed. -*Todd M. Hinnen, director for Combating Terrorism, National Security Council*[46]

Functional Analysis of Terrorist Financing. Terrorist organizations use a variety of alternative financing mechanisms to raise, move, and store their funds based on factors that are similar to other criminal organizations.[47] Terrorist organizations' goals are to operate in relative obscurity, use mechanisms involving close knit networks, and move their funds through industries and mechanisms that lack transparency and are poorly regulated.[48]

Due to the criminal nature of terrorist organizations and the lack of systematic data collection, analysis, and sharing of intelligence within the USG, the actual extent of alternative financing mechanisms by terrorist organizations is not known. In the past, U.S. law enforcement agencies, in particular the Federal Bureau of Investigation (FBI) which leads terrorist financing investigations, did not systematically collect and analyze data on alternative financing mechanisms.[49] This lack of data collection hindered the FBI and other IA from conducting systematic analysis of trends and patterns focused on terrorist financing. Without rigorous data collection, the FBI and, more importantly, the USG lacked the capability to conduct analyses that would have helped assess risk and prioritize U.S. efforts and limited resources. Moreover, despite an acknowledged need by most government agencies for further data collection, analysis, and the sharing of financial intelligence, few rigorous studies have been conducted in this area.[50]

Terrorist Organizational Structure. The U.S. can no longer afford to assume terrorist organizations use simple chain or line network structures (see Figure 1), with perfect circles that do not bleed or cross over into one another.[51]

The principal international terrorist organization today is best described as a *full-matrix* network (see Figure 2), the most highly developed network structure, in which all of its members are connected to, and can communicate with, all other members.[52] This full-matrix relationship between terrorists who belong to one or another group is what makes the threat of international terrorism so dangerous today. For example, while there are no known headquarters-to-headquarters links between Al Qaeda and Hezbollah, the two groups are known to have held senior level meetings over the past decade and to maintain ad hoc, person-to-person ties in the areas of training and logistical support.[53]

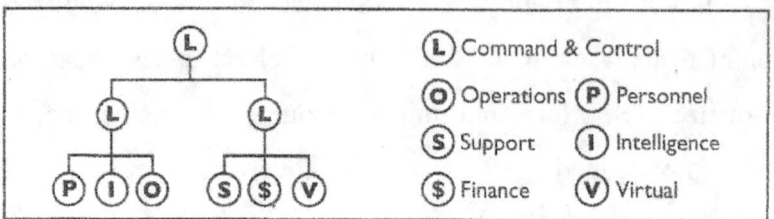

Figure 1. Example terrorist organization hierarchal structure. Adapted from the unpublished work of Major Grant Morris and the School of Advanced Military Studies Program Special Operations Elective.

Too often, the USG pigeonholes terrorists as members of one group or another, as if operatives carry membership cards around in their wallets. Today's terrorists are better defined as belonging to a *network of networks*, which is both informal and unstructured.[54] For instance, not every Al Qaeda operative has pledged an oath of allegiance (*bayat*) to Osama bin Laden, and many terrorists maintain affiliations with members of other terrorist groups and facilitate one another's activities.[55] Even though terrorist organizations tend to maintain the cellular structure at the tactical level for security purposes, one of their critical vulnerabilities at the operational and strategic level lies in the area of terrorist financing and logistical support due to the overlap and cooperation between terrorist groups and facilitators within their network of networks.

The DoD Dictionary of Military and Associated Terms defines *command and control* as "the exercise of authority and direction by a properly designated commander over assigned and attached forces in the accomplishment of the mission. Command and control functions are performed through an arrangement of personnel, equipment, communications, facilities, and procedures employed by a commander in planning, directing, coordinating, and controlling forces and operations in the accomplishment of the mission."[56] Unfortunately, terrorist networks do not use the same definition for command and control as the U.S. and many of its allies and partner nations. The implication of this fact is the increased need for the U.S. and its partners to maintain flexibility and perhaps even adapt their own command and control architecture to better enhance their disruption efforts.

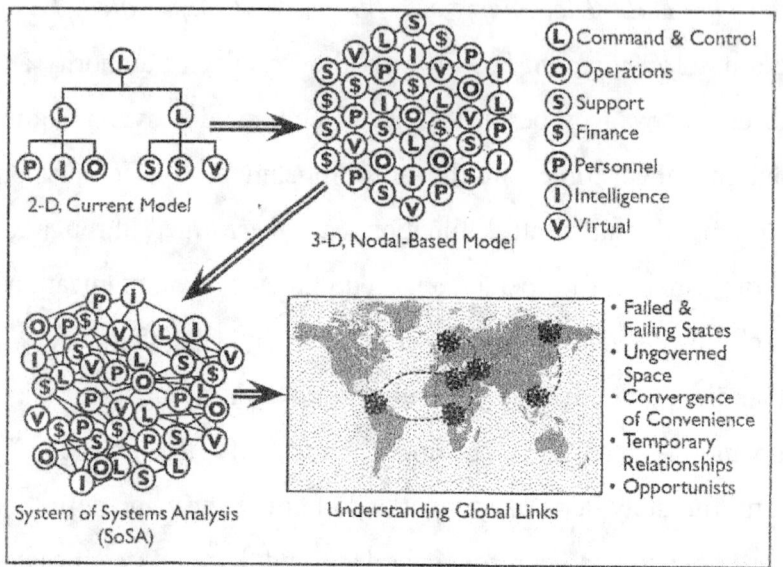

Figure 2. Example evolution to a full-matrix network. Adapted by the author from the unpublished work of Major Grant Morris and the School of Advanced Military Studies Program Special Operations Elective.

Full matrix, high tech. The full-matrix network represents the greatest potential threat to traditional hierarchical organizations and established governments like the U.S., especially as information technologies such as the Internet enhance communication among network members.[57] The full-matrix network's flat organizational architecture means that there may be no single leader. This is the case with Al Qaeda, contrary to popular belief, and it is why the organization is capable of conducting operations with or without the leadership of Osama bin Laden. Decision making and tactical operations are instead distributed among autonomous terrorist networks that share overarching principles, beliefs, and end states, such as the return of the caliphate.[58]

Maintenance of such shared principles, beliefs, and end states does, however, require the means for mutual consultation and consensus building among network nodes. Information technologies play a vital role in providing this means of information sharing among terrorist networks, but personal contact among node members is still necessary at times.[59]

Although information can be shared in many different ways and forms, one of the most common, safest, and effective means between terrorist networks is the Internet.[60] Terrorists use the Internet to develop and disseminate propaganda, recruit new members, raise and transfer funds, train members on weapons use and tactics, plan operations, and share documents and stored information with other terrorists throughout the world.[61] Terrorists can also access the vast wealth of information available on the Internet to facilitate operations, logistics, and financial support.

Sources and Movement of Terrorist Funds. Terrorist organizations raise funds through a variety of sources, including not-for-profit organizations, witting and unwitting; individual contributors, witting and unwitting; criminal activity; corporate contributors, witting and unwitting; operating businesses; state sponsors; and legal employment.[62] These funds provide the interchangeable, easily transportable means to secure all other forms of material support.

Once the funds are raised, terrorist organizations move the funds through several mechanisms, including cash couriers; alternative remittance systems "informal value transfer," such as hawalas and hundis; stored value cards; digital currency; Islamic banking systems; financial facilitators; trade and commodities-based methods; the Internet, through casinos and auctions; wire transfers; and formal international banking systems.[63] If the U.S. and its partners are going to succeed in the fight against terrorists, they must deprive terrorists of the material support they require by disrupting and monitoring the various funding sources and by interdicting the different movement mechanisms currently available. However, disrupting and monitoring terrorist funds without stifling the legal movement of funds remains a major challenge.

ORGANIZATIONS WITH MANDATES TO DISRUPT TERRORIST FINANCING

United States Organizations

The *National Security Strategy of the United States of America,* 2002 calls upon several different departments and agencies within the USG to disrupt terrorist financing by identifying and blocking the sources of their funding and denying them access to the international financial system.[64] To that end numerous organizations within the USG have lead, coordinating, or supporting roles in the effort to disrupt terrorist financing and are interconnected by a complex web of formal and informal relationships (see Appendix C for a more comprehensive listing).[65] This section focuses only on the major councils, departments, and agencies within the USG.[66]

National Security Council (NSC). The NSC is responsible for the overall coordination of the IA framework for combating terrorism, to include disrupting terrorist financing.[67] Under the NSC, a series of committees and working groups develop policy, share information and coordinate the response to terrorist threats against U.S. interests.[68] The NSC's Sub-Counterterrorism Security Group (CSG) on Terrorist Finance has the primary responsibility to ensure proper coordination of counterterrorism financing activities and information sharing among the IA, intelligence organizations, and law enforcement communities.[69] The NSC has several other Sub-Groups and offices that manage various programs and activities to combat terrorist financing abroad.[70]

The Treasury Department. Since June 1995, the Secretary of the Treasury has been responsible for identifying and blocking terrorist funds within the U.S. and its jurisdiction.[71] In addition, a number of Treasury Department offices work with other federal agencies to implement key statutory provisions of the Currency and Foreign Transactions Reporting Act (commonly referred to as the Bank Secrecy Act, BSA of 1970) and the Uniting and Strengthening America by Providing Appropriate Tools Required to Intercept and Obstruct Terrorism Act of 2001 (better known as the USA Patriot Act), and to enhance information sharing among intelligence, law enforcement, and financial institutions.[72]

The primary office within the Treasury Department that is involved in the effort to disrupt terrorist financing is the Office of Terrorism and Financial Intelligence (TFI). The TFI is comprised of: a) the Office of Terrorist Financing, b) the Office of Intelligence and Analysis, c) the Office of Foreign Asset Control, d) the Financial Crimes Enforcement Network, and e) the Treasury Executive Office for Asset Forfeiture and Treasury Forfeiture Fund.[73] In addition, the Treasury Department has several other offices that manage various programs and activities to combat terrorist financing abroad.[74]

The Department of State (DoS). The DoS serves as the USG's lead agency in its efforts to combat terrorism overseas. To safeguard the international financial system against terrorist financing and money laundering, the DoS focuses on three areas:

    a. Designation, by blocking assets and cutting off worldwide channels of terrorist financing

    b. Standard setting, by establishing internationally accepted standards

    c. Capacity and coalition building, by building the technical capacity and political will to ensure global compliance with international standards.[75]

Within the DoS, the Office of the Coordinator for Counterterrorism (S/CT) and the Bureau of International Narcotics and Law Enforcement Affairs (INL) have the primary responsibility for coordinating capacity building abroad to disrupt terrorist financing, while the Bureau of Economic, Energy, and Business Affairs (EEB) has primary responsibility for international coalition building.[76] In addition,

DoS has several other bureaus and offices that manage various programs and activities that help combat terrorist financing.[77]

The Department of Justice (DoJ). The DoJ has the lead responsibility for investigating and prosecuting terrorist acts, including all forms of material support to terrorist organizations.[78] Within the DoJ, the FBI has the lead role for law enforcement and criminal matters related to terrorism.[79] The two major organizations within the DoJ that are involved in disrupting terrorist financing are the Terrorist Financing Unit (TFU) and the Terrorist Financing Operations Section (TFOS), which falls under the FBI.[80]

Department of Homeland Security (DHS). DHS has a supporting role in tracking terrorist financing and conducting related investigations within the U.S. and select overseas activities.[81] The major organization within the DHS that is involved in disrupting terrorist financing is the Bureau of Immigration and Customs Enforcement (ICE).[82]

The Department of Defense. The DoD has a supporting role within the USG in the fight against terrorist financing. Accordingly, the DoD has broadened its nonkinetic efforts to include the disruption of threat financing. While terrorist financing concentrates on organizations, networks, cells, and individuals directly linked to terrorism, and is the primary focus of this paper, it is only one of the five areas within threat financing. Threat financing is a broader-based concept that includes Weapons of Mass Destruction/Effects (WMD/E) funding, terrorist financing, narcotics trafficking, organized crime, and human trafficking.[83]

Within the DoD, the United States Special Operations Command (USSOCOM) has been designated the executive agent for synchronizing the GWOT, which includes disrupting and defeating threat finances.[84] The other two major organizations within the DoD that facilitate the disruption of terrorist finances are the geographic combatant commands (GCCs), through Threat Finance Exploitation Units (TFEUs), and various Combat Support Agencies, such as the Defense Intelligence Agency (DIA), through the Joint Intelligence Task Force-Combating Terrorism (JITF-CT).

    a. **USSOCOM.** As the supported combatant command for the GWOT, USSOCOM synchronizes the counterterrorism plans of the five GCCs.[85] USSOCOM also plans and executes combat missions against terrorist organizations as the supported Command, while maintaining the role of force provider to the other GCCs.[86] With regard to terrorist financing,

USSOCOM's Threat Finance Exploitation Branch has the lead for synchronizing efforts against threat finances.

b. **Geographic Combatant Commands.** The GCCs are currently assessing the ability of terrorists and insurgents to finance operations and the effectiveness of the U.S. military efforts to deny resources to terrorist organizations. Initial data from these assessments indicate that the DoD, while enjoying some successes in analyzing and disrupting the funds of terrorists and insurgents, is progressing slowly in combating terrorist financing on a global scale.[87] Currently, U.S. Central Command (USCENTCOM), U.S. European Command (USEUCOM), U.S. Northern Command (USNORTHCOM), U.S. Pacific Command (USPACOM), and U.S. Southern Command (USSOUTHCOM) are operating TFEUs that work with DoD and non-DoD intelligence, law enforcement, and regulatory agencies to detect financial support networks; collect, process and analyze information; and target, disrupt, or destroy financial systems and networks, which support activities that threaten U.S. interests.[88]

Not all GCCs call their TF Exploitation entity a TFEU. For instance USSOCOM calls its entity a TF Exploitation Branch, but each GCC has an entity that analyzes and exploits financial intelligence. Each of the TF Exploitation entities has a somewhat different focus that is based on their region. For example, USSOUTHCOM is more focused on the narcotics trafficking portion of TF, whereas USCENTCOM is focused more on the terrorists and insurgents. Each of the TF Exploitation entities are resourced, manned, and utilized to varying degrees based on the emphasis that is placed on their importance by the GCC, and not all TF Exploitation entities operate at the same level of proficiency.

International Organizations

Terrorist financing networks are global, so efforts to identify and disrupt terrorist access to funds must also be global.[89] Moreover, because the overwhelming majority of terrorist funds are outside U.S. jurisdiction, the U.S. has entered into several agreements to improve and facilitate international organizations' counterterrorism efforts.[90] International organizations can be grouped into four main categories: international standard setters, international capacity builders, regional entities, and industry-sector standard setters (see Appendix D for a more comprehensive listing).[91]

International Standard Setters

United Nations. The United Nations is one of the key international entities in the fight against terrorist organizations and networks. The single biggest role conducted by the United Nations with regard to terrorist financing is the imposition and enforcement of international financial sanctions through the designation lists maintained under UNSCR 1267 and 1617.[92] In addition, the United Nations provides member states with numerous forms of assistance for their counterterrorism efforts through the contributions of various departments, programs, and specialized agencies.[93] On 8 September, 2006, the United Nations began a new phase in its counterterrorism efforts by adopting the Global Counterterrorism Strategy, which serves as a common platform to bring together the counterterrorism efforts of the various United Nations departments, programs, and specialized agencies into a common, coherent, and more focused framework.[94] Although the United Nations consists of numerous departments and specialized agencies, the Counterterrorism Implementation Task Force (CTITF) and the Counterterrorism Committee (CTC) have the largest roles in disrupting terrorist finances.[95]

Financial Action Task Force. The FATF consists of 33 member countries and 2 regional organizations. It is one of the preeminent international bodies dedicated to developing, promoting, and assessing legal and regulatory standards and policies to combat money laundering and terrorist financing.[96] FATF's most notable contributions against terrorism include two fundamental documents:

    a. *The FATF Forty Recommendations on Money Laundering*, a set of international standards for countries to establish an effective anti-money-laundering regime

    b. *Nine Special Recommendations on Terrorist Financing*, which has become the international standard for evaluating a state's antiterrorist financing laws.[97]

In addition, FATF established a Non-Cooperative Countries and Territories (NCCT) list of those countries that fail to meet internationally recognized standards and serve as terrorist money laundering havens, monitors member progress in implementing anti-moneylaundering measures, conducts mutual evaluations of its member countries and jurisdictions, and reports on money laundering trends and techniques.[98]

International Capacity Builders

Egmont Group. The Egmont Group is an international body, comprised of 101 financial intelligence units (FIUs), that fosters improved communications, information sharing, and training coordination worldwide in the fight against money laundering and terrorist financing.[99] The FIUs work collectively to eliminate impediments to information sharing, promote the reporting of terrorist financing as a suspicious activity to FIUs, and undertake joint studies on money laundering and terrorist financing vulnerabilities. They also improve expertise and capabilities of law enforcement personnel and agencies, and they expand and create a systematic exchange of financial intelligence information.[100]

The International Criminal Police Organization (INTERPOL). INTERPOL is the world's largest international police organization, with 186 member countries that facilitate cross border police cooperation. INTERPOL also supports and assists all organizations, authorities, and services whose mission is to prevent or combat international crime.[101] With regard to combating financial crimes, INTERPOL's primary focus is on payment cards, money laundering, intellectual property crime, currency counterfeiting, and new technologies, all of which can be used by terrorist organizations to fund their operations.[102] Within INTERPOL, the Fusion Task Force (FTF) has the lead for conducting antiterrorism efforts. The FTF's primary objectives include identifying active terrorist groups and their members; soliciting, collecting, and sharing information and intelligence; providing analytical support; and enhancing the capacity of member countries to address the threats of terrorism and organized crime.[103]

Weaknesses within the U.S. and International Organizational Framework

There are four major weaknesses within the U.S. and international organizational framework:

a. No organization has both the mandate and funding authority to coordinate and direct the actions of all USG agencies against terrorist organizations.

b. Information sharing is predicated on a *need to know* versus a *need to share* basis within the U.S. and international community.

c. No integrated and collaborative communications network exists within the U.S. or between its allies and partner nations.

d. An insufficient effort made to maximize information between the collector, analyst, and end user and the inability to utilize a commonly understood language.

LEGAL CONSIDERATIONS

In the fight against terrorist financing, it is critical to address the authority of international organizations for several reasons. First, most of the funds supporting terrorist organizations are not under the control or jurisdiction of the U.S. Therefore, the U.S. must internationalize its initiatives.[104] Second, international organizations have a tremendous sphere of influence, so by influencing and supporting various international conventions and resolutions the U.S. can protect its own interests through the efforts of various other countries around the world.[105] Finally, the U.S. has ratified all thirteen international conventions relating to terrorism, which means U.S. domestic laws must be in compliance with and support these international conventions.[106]

International conventions and resolutions designed to disrupt the flow of terrorist financing are discussed below in two parts: international conventions and United Nations Security Council Resolutions (see Appendix E for a more comprehensive listing). Following the international conventions and resolutions, U.S. laws and federal regulations are discussed.

International Conventions

International conventions serve an important role in coordinating the counterterrorism efforts and establishing legal norms within the various ratifying states around the world. Two international conventions that are important in facilitating the disruption of terrorist financing are the International Convention for the Suppression of the Financing of Terrorism and the International Convention against Transnational Organized Crime.

International Convention for the Suppression of the Financing of Terrorism, 1999. This convention established terrorist financing as a distinct offense, which is constituted by directly or indirectly, unlawfully and willfully, providing or collecting funds with the intent that they should be used or in the knowledge that they are to be used, in full or in part, to carry out an offense described in any one of the other twelve United Nations counterterrorist treaties, or to commit any other violent act with the intent of intimidating a population or compelling a government to act in a certain manner. The convention contains four primary obligations that a) criminalize the provision or collection of funds for terrorists; b) prohibit the provision of funds, assets or financial services to terrorists; c) freeze without delay terrorist funds or other assets; and d) establish adequate identification and reporting procedures for financial institutions. In addition, the convention requires ratifying countries to criminalize terrorism, terrorist organizations, and terrorist acts and encourages member states to implement measures that are consistent with FATF recommendations.[107]

International Convention Against Transnational Organized Crime, 2000. Although not one of the thirteen United Nations conventions that specifically address terrorism, this convention can be used as an effective tool to disrupt terrorist financing. Member states that have ratified the convention are required to establish within their domestic laws four criminal offenses: participation in an organized criminal group, money laundering, corruption, and obstruction of justice.[108] The convention also obligates ratifying countries to:

a. Criminalize all serious crimes as predicate offenses of money laundering, whether committed within or outside of the country, and permits the required criminal knowledge or intent to be inferred from objective facts.

b. Establish regulatory regimes to deter and detect all forms of money laundering, including customer identification, record keeping, and reporting of suspicious transactions.

c. Authorize the cooperation and exchange of information among administrative, regulatory, law enforcement, and other authorities, both domestically and internationally.

d. Establish a financial intelligence unit to collect, analyze, and disseminate information.

e. Promote international cooperation.[109]

United Nations Security Resolutions

The USG, with the DoS in the lead, maintains a working relationship with the United Nations to develop and support numerous UNSCRs (United Nations Security Council Resolutions) such as 1267, 1269, 1373, 1617, 1730, and 1735, that have helped give international momentum and legitimacy to the global effort against terrorist financing.[110] This is extremely important because most of the assets making their way to terrorist organizations are not under U.S. control or jurisdiction, and when an individual or organization, such as Al Qaeda, is included on the United Nations sanctions list, all 191 United Nations member states are obligated to implement the sanctions, such as freezing the assets.[111]

UNSCR 1267, 1999. UNSCR 1267 obligates member states to freeze assets of individuals and organizations associated with Osama bin Laden, members of Al Qaeda or the Taliban that are included on the consolidated list maintained and regularly updated by the United Nations 1267 Sanctions Committee.[112] UNSCR 1267 is also one of the implementing authorities for EO 13224.[113]

UNSCR 1269, 1999. UNSCR 1269 calls on member states to implement the international antiterrorist conventions to which they are a party. Although the Security Council specifically referred to terrorist financing" for the first time in UNSCR 1269, it was not in the context of state-sponsored terrorism. However, General Assembly Resolution 49/60 clearly implicated state entities directly in such financing by acts and omissions such as sheltering, facilitating, funding, and failing to adopt suppressive measures.[114]

UNSCR 1373, 2001. UNSCR 1373 is the broadest of the UNSCRs and obligates member states to:
  a. Criminalize actions that finance terrorism.
  b. Prevent and suppress terrorist financing, and freeze funds and other financial assets or economic resources of persons who commit or attempt to commit terrorist acts.
  c. Prohibit active or passive assistance to terrorists.

d. Cooperate with other countries in criminal investigations and share information with regard to planned terrorist acts.[115]

UNSCR 1617, 2005. UNSCR 1617 extended sanctions against Al Qaeda, Osama bin Laden, and the Taliban, and it strengthened previous related resolutions. This resolution:

a. Extended the mandate of the 1267 Sanctions Committee's Monitoring Team.

b. Clarified what constitutes association with Al Qaeda.

c. Strongly urged all member states to implement the comprehensive international standards embodied in the FATF Forty Recommendations on Money Laundering and Nine Special Recommendations on Terrorist Financing.

d. Requested the Secretary General increase cooperation between the United Nations and INTERPOL in order to provide the United Nations 1267 Committee with better tools to fulfill its mandate.

e. Urged member states to ensure that stolen and lost passports and other travel documents were invalidated as soon as possible, as well as to share information on those documents with other member states through the INTERPOL database.[116]

UNSCR 1730 (2006). UNSCR 1730 expanded on UNSCR 1617 and added an element of due process to designation mechanism. UNSCR 1730:

a. Emphasizes that sanctions are an important tool in the maintenance and restoration of international peace and security.

b. Adopts delisting procedures and requests the Secretary-General establish, within the Secretariat (Security Council Subsidiary Organs Branch), a focal point to receive delisting requests and to perform the tasks described in the annex to UNSCR 1730.

c. Directs the sanctions committees established by the Security Council, including those established pursuant to resolution 1718 (2006), 1636 (2005), 1591 (2005), 1572 (2004), 1533 (2004), 1521 (2005), 1518 (2003), 1267 (1999), 1132 (1997), 918 (1994), and 751 (1992) to revise their guidelines accordingly.[117]

UNSCR 1735 (2006). UNSCR 1735 is a rollover of UNSCR 1617, reaffirming 1267, 1373, 1617, standardizing listing procedures through the use of cover sheet and statement of case. UNSCR 1735 expresses deep concern about the criminal misuse of the Internet and the nature of the threat, particularly the ways in which terrorist ideologies are promoted by Al Qaeda, Osama bin Laden, and the Taliban, and other individuals, groups, undertakings, and entities associated with them, in furtherance of terrorist acts. In addition, UNSCR 1735 freezes the funds and other financial assets or economic resources of these individuals, groups, undertakings and entities, including funds derived from property owned or controlled, directly or indirectly, by them or by persons acting on their behalf or at their direction, and ensures that neither these nor any other funds, financial assets or economic resources are made available, directly or indirectly, for such persons' benefit, or by their nationals or by persons within their territory.[118]

U.S. Laws and Federal Regulations

U.S. laws, federal regulations and policies designed to disrupt the flow of terrorist financing and are discussed in three parts: sanction-focused laws, banking-focused laws, and federal regulations (see Appendix F for a more comprehensive listing).[119]

U.S. Sanction-Focused Laws

Two important sanction-focused laws facilitate the disruption of terrorist financing: the International Emergency Economic

Powers Act and the Antiterrorism and Effective Death Penalty Act.

International Emergency Economic Powers Act (IEEPA), 1977. The IEEPA falls under the provisions of the National Emergencies Act and authorizes the President of the United States (POTUS) to deal with any unusual and extraordinary threat to the national security, foreign policy, or economy of the U.S., which has its source in whole or substantial part outside the U.S., if the POTUS declares a national emergency with respect to such a threat.[120] It further authorizes the POTUS, after such a declaration, to block transactions and freeze assets to deal with the stated threat. In the event of an actual attack on the U.S., the POTUS can also confiscate property connected with a country, group, or person that aided in the attack.[121]

Antiterrorism and Effective Death Penalty Act (AEDPA), 1996. The AEDPA was the product of legislative efforts stretching back well over a decade. It was energized in part by the tragedies in Oklahoma City and at the World Trade Center and serves as the empowering statute for FTO designation.[122] The AEDPA has several important antiterrorist measures:

  a. Makes membership in a designated terrorist organization a basis for the denial of a visa to enter the U.S.

b. Makes illegal-alien terrorists excludable rather than deportable, wherever and whenever they are apprehended.

c. Establishes special deportation procedures for aliens believed to be engaged in terrorist activities when there is evidence of a classified nature to support the allegation.

d. Allows the Attorney General to request assistance from the DoD in cases involving WMD.

e. Authorizes funds to establish a counterterrorism center, which eventually became the National Counterterrorism Center (NCTC).[123]

The AEDPA contains two specific provisions that address terrorist financing:

a. Bans material support (excluding medical and religious materials) that is knowingly given to foreign organizations designated as terrorist by the Secretary of State.

b. Closes a loophole in the judicial system that permitted groups to raise money for terrorist organizations.[124]

U.S. Banking-Focused Laws

Two banking focused laws that are important in facilitating the disruption of terrorist financing are the Currency and Foreign Transactions Reporting Act and the Uniting and Strengthening America by Providing Appropriate Tools

Required to Intercept and Obstruct Terrorism Act (USA Patriot Act).

Currency and Foreign Transactions Reporting Act, 1970. The Currency and Foreign Transactions Reporting Act, otherwise known as the Bank Secrecy Act (BSA), was designed to help identify the source, volume, and movement of currency and other monetary instruments into or out of the U.S.[125] The central purpose of the BSA is to fight money laundering, terrorist financing, and other illicit financing activities. Today more than 170 crimes are listed in the federal money laundering statutes. They range from drug trafficking, gunrunning, murder for hire, and fraud, to acts of terrorism.[126]

USA Patriot Act, 2001. This act was passed after the attacks of 9/11 and greatly expanded the authority and investigative tools of law enforcement agencies to disrupt terrorist activities at home and abroad.[127] The USA Patriot Act enhances the U.S. ability to combat terrorist financing and money laundering in several ways:

a. Expanding anti-money-laundering compliance program requirements of organizations, such as broker-dealers and casinos

b. Facilitating access to records and requiring banks to respond to requests for information within 120 hours

c. Requiring regulatory agencies to evaluate an institution's anti-money laundering (AML) record when considering bank mergers, acquisitions, and other applications for business combinations

d. Providing the Secretary of the Treasury with the authority to impose "special measures" on jurisdictions, institutions, or transactions that are of "primary money-laundering concern." 128

U.S. Federal Regulations

EO 13224. The USG's primary and most public tool in the fight against terrorist financing is EO 13224.[129] EO 13224 provides a means of disrupting the financial support network for terrorists and terrorist organizations by authorizing the USG to designate and block the assets of foreign individuals and entities that commit, or pose a significant risk of committing, acts of terrorism.[130] In addition, the order authorizes the USG to block the assets of individuals and entities that provide support, services, or assistance to, or otherwise associate with, terrorists and terrorist organizations designated under the order, as well as their subsidiaries, front organizations, agents, and associates.[131] EO 13224 serves as an outstanding example of leveraging international efforts to support U.S. interests. In 2005, there were 300 individuals and entities designated by the USG pursuant to EO 13224 that were listed on the UNSCR 1267/1617 Consolidated List.[132]

DoD Directives. As stated in Chapter 1, DoD has no defined authorities under U.S. law and regulations nor does DoD have an overarching policy that addresses threat finance. However, DoD derives its roles and responsibilities from the National Strategy for Combating Terrorism, the National Implementation Plan (NIP), and various other classified national action plans.

RECOMMENDATIONS AND DESIRED EFFECTS

Designate an Organization with the Mandate and Funding Authority to Direct Actions

Issue. Currently there is no overarching organization with the mandate and funding authority to direct the actions of the IA against terrorist organizations.

Discussion. The NSC has the authority to coordinate actions among the IA. What the NSC does not have is the authority to:

a. Mandate actions when justifiable differences and priorities occur within the IA.

b. Mandate strategic alignment of efforts and resources.

c. Allocate additional resources to facilitate IA requirements when necessary.[133]

In addition, the NCTC serves as the primary organization in the USG for integrating and analyzing all intelligence pertaining to terrorism and counterterrorism activities, conducting strategic operational planning by integrating all instruments of national power, and coordinating and monitoring counterterrorism plans and activities between the various government agencies.[134] Although the NCTC has worked to integrate the various intelligence agencies' efforts and coordinate the various counterterrorism plans and activities within the USG, those efforts represent only one piece of the solution.

Neither the NSC nor NCTC has the mandate and funding authority to provide a fully integrated and resourced holistic approach to maximize U.S. efforts in disrupting terrorist organizations. The current system is predicated on the various IA putting aside legitimate differences with respect to focus, priorities, resources, and mission requirements and working together in a collegial manner to accomplish what is often a poorly orchestrated and resourced effort. While the current system has merit, it has a tendency to rely heavily on force of personality and informal relationships between the various organizations rather than on any mandated structural mechanism to achieve its end state. The disruption of terrorist finances must be addressed within the overarching context of threat finance, and threat finance must be integrated and resourced as part of a holistic approach in the fight against terrorist organizations.

Currently the U.S. operates under a system in which the NSC has the authority to coordinate the various efforts of organizations such as CIA, DHS, DoJ, FBI, DoD, Treasury Department, and NCTC, as well as representatives of other departments or agencies as needed. Nonetheless, the various IA all work towards their own specific goals and agendas without an overarching organization directing their efforts. To be successful the U.S. must address the problem of terrorism under the guidance and leadership of one overarching organization that has the mandate and funding authority to direct all activities' and agencies' actions against terrorist organizations.

Recommendations

Increase National Security Council authority. The NSC should be given legislative authority to:

a. Direct actions.

b. Establish funding priorities.

c. Develop an integrated U.S. strategy.

d. Establish accountability mechanisms.

e. Allocate additional resources as needed.

Delegate to the Sub-Counterterrorism Security Group. The NSC should accomplish these new mandates through the Sub-CSG.

Implement Counterterrorism Security Group. The CSG should:

a. Rename the Sub-CSG on Terrorist Finance to the Sub-CSG on Threat Finance.

b. Designate the Sub-CSG on Threat Finance as the lead organization against Threat Finance.

c. Establish a working group or fusion center that allows all the organizations of the IA, law enforcement, and banking industry to integrate and deconflict their actions before being brought up to the Sub-CSG level.

Desired Effect

The desired effect is the establishment of one organization with the mandate and funding authority to direct and leverage the various assets within the U.S. in concert with one another to achieve a synergistic and well-orchestrated end state. These recommendations would help facilitate not only alignment of the disparate organizations and agencies but also foreign policy guidance, diplomatic engagement, and training and technical assistance to foreign countries. This, in turn, will:

a. Enhance disruption of and risk to terrorist organizations worldwide.

b. Increase the security of U.S. citizens.

c. Protect U.S. interests at home and abroad.

Enhanced Multilateral Information and Intelligence Sharing

Issue. The current U.S. information and intelligence sharing framework is predicated on the concept of *need to know* versus *need to share*.

Discussion. Multilateral information sharing is critical to the U.S. efforts against terrorist organizations. Since 9/11, most of the important U.S. successes against terrorist organizations have been made possible through effective multilateral partnerships. Continued success depends on the actions of a powerful coalition of nations and industry enhancing the flow of information and intelligence between one another. While much of the information the intelligence community produces can be of significant value in the fight against terrorist organizations, the value will not be fully realized or maximized until multilateral efforts are made to filter, analyze, and disseminate the information to those organizations that can make the best use of the information in a timely manner.[135] While great strides have been made to enhance the sharing of information among the IA since 9/11, the U.S. still has a lot of room for improvement when it comes to obtaining, analyzing, and disseminating information in a timely fashion, especially with respect to the private sector entities, allies, and partner nations.

There are times when information should not be shared in a multilateral fashion due to political, operational, and various security reasons, these reasons should be treated as the exception to the rule rather than the norm. With respect to threat finance, information sharing predicated on a *need to know* mentality actually increases risk. For instance, members of the USG interact weekly with various other nations and private industries around the world who ask to see the facts that substantiate the U.S. case for designating a group as a terrorist organization or for nominating an organization for inclusion on the UNSCR 1267/1617 Consolidated List. Unfortunately, these questions are often not answered to the satisfaction of the questioning nation based on the unwillingness or inability of the U.S. to share the pertinent information that substantiates its case.[136] Due to the fact that the country does not understand the reasons for designation, they are often less likely to support the U.S. designation, especially when the nation views the organization in question as a legitimate and often beneficial organization and has no available information or intelligence to the contrary.

Recommendations

Implement *Need to Share*. The U.S. should pass applicable laws, treaties, arrangements, or other mechanisms that would allow and encourage a change in its information and intelligence sharing framework from a *need to know* to a *need to share* mentality. Specifically, legislation, treaties, arrangements, or other mechanisms should expand the language found in EO 13356: *Strengthening the Sharing of Terrorism Information to Protect Americans,* 2004 and EO 13388: *Further Strengthening the Sharing of Terrorism Information to Protect Americans,* 2005 to cover allies and partner nations. This would allow the U.S. to:

a. Grant access to terrorism information and intelligence to the heads of various agencies, organizations, and nations that have counterterrorism functions and provide a standardized method for sharing information and intelligence.

b. Cooperate in the development and facilitate the production of reports based on terrorism information with contents and formats that permit maximum dissemination.

c. Provide a common standard for the sharing of terrorism information by agencies within the intelligence community (IC).

In addition, the U.S. could improve information and intelligence sharing by:

a. Requiring, at the outset of the intelligence collection and analysis process, the creation of records and reporting for both raw and processed information, including, for example, metadata and content in such a manner that sources and methods are protected so that the information can be distributed at lower classification levels, and by creating unclassified versions for distribution whenever possible

b. Requiring records and reports related to terrorism information to be produced with multiple versions at an unclassified level and at varying levels of classification, e.g., on an electronic tear line basis, allowing varying degrees of access

c. Requiring terrorism information to be shared free of originator controls

d. Minimizing the applicability of information compartmentalization systems to terrorism information

e. Establishing appropriate arrangements that provide incentives for, and hold personnel accountable for, increased sharing of terrorism information consistent with requirements of the Nation's security.[137]

Improve information sharing. Legislation should be passed to expand the role of the Program Manager Information Sharing Environment (PIMSE) to include allies and partner nations. PIMSE has made headway with regard to improving terrorism information sharing between federal, state, local, and tribal entities and is progressing toward incorporating private sector entities. However, the U.S. must expand its efforts to facilitate information sharing with foreign governments. In addition, legislation should be passed to modify the Intelligence Reform and Terrorism Prevention Act (IRTPA), 2004 with respect to NCTC by adding purely domestic terrorist groups to the language.

Improve data acquisition. Legislation should be passed that facilitates and streamlines acquisition of terrorism information data. The current system is often a legally and bureaucratically cumbersome process, wherein Secretary-level government officials frequently must approve the data transfer.[138] Without timely and accurate passage of information the U.S. is only hampering its efforts and creating additional seams for terrorists to exploit.

Desired Effect

The desired effect is a proactive information and intelligence sharing framework predicated on a *need to share* mentality. Through multilateral cooperation the U.S. will enhance the ability of its allies and partner nations across the globe to:

a. Secure critical infrastructures

b. Enhance the disruption and risk to terrorist organizations worldwide

c. Deny terrorist funding and freedom of movement

d. Deny terrorists access to WMD/E and safe havens in ungoverned spaces around the world.

An Integrated and Collaborative Information and Intelligence Sharing Network

Issue. Currently there is no integrated and collaborative information and intelligence sharing network within the U.S. between the IA, law enforcement, private sector, allies, and partner nations.

Discussion. While there are numerous types of information and intelligence sharing architectures in existence, none of the current systems allow for integrated and collaborative information and intelligence sharing between the IA, law enforcement, private sector, allies, and partner nations.[139] Some progress has been made over the past five years, especially with the creation of NCTC Online (NOL), but most of the current systems are disjointed and stovepiped and still do not maximize timely information and intelligence sharing.

One of the keys to success in the effort to disrupt terrorist organizations is the ability of IA, law enforcement, private sector, allies, and partner nations to conduct integrated and collaborative efforts over a network that is secure, flexible, and allows for timely passage of information, while being robust enough to meet evolving command, control, communications, and computer requirements.

Recommendation

The U.S. should create an integrated and collaborative information and intelligence sharing network among the IA, law enforcement, private sector, allies, and partner nations called the Worldwide Information and Intelligence Network (WIIN) (see Appendix G for a more comprehensive explanation).[140] WIIN would create an integrated and collaborative international online community against terrorism that could be used to:

a. Maximize the use of limited resources.

b. Filter, analyze, and disseminate practical information in a timely manner using tear lines for those organizations that can best use the information.

c. Create access to raw, current, and finished intelligence products.

d. Facilitate development of international standards with regard to intelligence reporting, legal authorities, law enforcement, banking, definitions and terms, and technical and training assistance.

e. Increase law enforcement ability to prevent, investigate, and prosecute terrorist organizations through the exchange of information between law enforcement, security agencies, and private sector organizations.

f. Create a repository for standardized data points on patterns, techniques and mechanisms that would enhance modeling of terrorist organizations and increase international understanding of the patterns and behaviors of terrorist organizations.

g. Facilitate the development of metrics to measure the effects of current counterterrorism efforts.

h. Help create an effective risk-based holistic screening tool.

i. Create a service-oriented architecture to separate data from applications and improve the integration of legacy capabilities.

The advantages of WIIN are that:

a. The Internet is used as the coordination backbone.

b. Provides a platform for integrated collaboration and communications from the Unclassified to Top Secret (TS)/Sensitive Compartmented Information (SCI) levels.

c. All communication systems used in the system comply with NSA and Communications Security Establishment (CSE) standards for Type 1 encryption.

d. All traffic from site to site is encrypted in accordance with NSA guidelines using Type 1 encryption devices.

e. Does not require additional hardware at the individual user level.

f. It is deployable.

g. Provides capabilities for file sharing and transfer, e-mail, Web conferencing with Voice over IP (VoIP), chat, instant messaging, Web-based information management (which in turn allows publishing and compartmentalization of the system), and providing a Common Operational Picture (COP) at a package cost of $1,200,000 per server with a tail of $250,000 per year as designed.

While WIIN would create a complicated balance of legal, technical, security, and policy matters that would need to be resolved, and a massive quantity of information that would need to be filtered, the gains would far outweigh the risks and challenges involved. Since various organizations around the world hold different pieces of the terrorist finance puzzle, it is critical for the U.S. to have the ability to access information and intelligence in its entirety if it hopes to create a complete picture against which to allocate its resources.

Desired Effect

The desired effect is an integrated collaborative network that enhances information and intelligence sharing among the IA, law enforcement, private sector, allies, and partner nations from the Unclassified to TS/SCI level on a *need to share* basis. This, in turn, will enhance the disruption and risk to terrorist organizations worldwide, increase the security of U.S. citizens, and protect U.S. interests at home and abroad.

DoD Policy and Way Ahead

Issue. Currently, the DoD has neither policy nor way ahead on how to facilitate and integrate its threat finance efforts with regard to the IA, law enforcement, private sector, allies, and partner nations.

Discussion. While the DoD derives its threat finance roles and responsibilities from the National Strategy for Combating Terrorism (NSCT), 2006, the NIP, and various other national actions plans, these strategies and plans do not constitute a DoD threat finance policy or way ahead. The DoD has also developed the National Military Strategic Plan for the War on Terrorism (NMSP-WOT), 2006, and several other classified plans, execution orders, and assessments to combat terrorism, but these documents do not constitute a policy or way ahead with respect to threat finance, either.

Other threat finance areas that DoD should address to maximize its capabilities and resources to better protect U.S. interests at home and abroad include developing:

a. Refined threat finance organizational structure

b. Types of actions that could be conducted in support of the IA, law enforcement, allies, and partner nations

c. Doctrine, organization, training, material, leadership, facilities, and personnel (DOTMLFP) requirements

d. Cadre of experts in the field of threat finance and a method for tracking these experts within DoD

e. Comprehensive education and training program

f. Baseline list of equipment requirements

g. Tactics, techniques, and procedures

h. New threat finance doctrine, as well as an integration of current threat finance concepts into current doctrine

i. Method that would synchronize the DoD terrorist list with the IA

j. Synchronization method that broadens DoD focus from GCC level to the global level and that allows DoD to speak with one voice when interacting with IA, law enforcement, private sector, allies, and partner nations at the strategic level

k. Better relationships with the IA, law enforcement, private sector, allies, and partner nations to enhance DoD understanding of their equities, objectives, and requirements. DoD needs to place more emphasis and resources behind its efforts.

The first NMSP-WOT, 2006 GWOT military strategic objective listed is to deny terrorists the resources they need to operate and survive.[141] If this is truly the DoD number one strategic objective, then DoD should allocate additional resources accordingly.

Recommendations

Develop policy. The first recommendation is for DoD to develop a clear and well thought out policy and way ahead through a collaborative effort between the Secretary of Defense, Under Secretary of Defense for Policy, Assistant Secretary of Defense for Special Operations and Low Intensity Conflict (ASD SO/LIC), Joint Chiefs of Staff, unified combatant commands, combat support agencies (CSA), IA, law enforcement, private sector, allies, and partner nations.[142]

The Under Secretary of Defense for Policy should develop, coordinate, and oversee the implementation of DoD policy for threat finance planning, preparation, coordination, implementation, support, and lessons learned, and represent DoD at the Sub-CSG on Terrorist Finance.

The ASD SO/LIC should:

a. Serve as the principal staff assistant and civilian advisor to the Secretary of Defense and the Undersecretary of Defense for Policy on threat finance.

b. Establish and promulgate goals and objectives, policy guidance, and recommendations on threat finance.

c. Determine threat finance requirements in accordance with DoD threat finance policy and strategic guidance, once it is developed.

d. Promulgate policy and provide policy guidance and recommendations on DoD support to other government agencies.

e. Coordinate the development of a plan of action and milestones (POAM)

f. Coordinate and review DoD progress toward developing a flexible and fully integrated threat finance architecture.

g. Serve as the DoD focal point for integrating DOTMLFP requirements.

h. Convene a threat finance coordination group to develop, review, and recommend policy level actions which would serve to integrate the actions of various DoD entities.

The Joint Chiefs of Staff should:

a. Provide advice to the Secretary of Defense on military aspects of threat finance.

b. Coordinate implementation of a threat finance policy and DOTMLFP requirements.

c. Ensure that the Joint Requirements Oversight Council (JROC) reviews threat finance annual requirements.

Each of the unified combatant commands and defense agencies should develop a threat finance capability with clearly delineated roles and responsibilities that are integrated with a Joint and Interagency Coordination Group (JIACG) tailored to meet the requirements and challenges of their organizations. Such actions would result in improved interagency cooperation and operational effectiveness at the operational and tactical level. If the unified combatant command or defense agency does not have a JIACG or a Joint Interagency Task Force, then at a minimum DoS and the Treasury Department should exchange liaison officers (LNOs) and increase IA assignments to enhance threat finance coordination and interoperability.

Finally, USSOCOM should be appointed as the synchronizing entity within DoD to promote interoperability with regard to equipment requirements; education and training; doctrinal development and integration; tactics, techniques, and procedures development and integration; developing and advancing threat finance capabilities; and terrorist designation integration and synchronization between the DoD and the IA by adopting the NCTC tiered threat priority construct.

This first recommendation is by no means a complete solution to the problem and does not address several of the current problems related to threat finance. For instance, the roles for several of the Under Secretary and Assistant Secretary positions, such as the Under Secretary of Defense for Intelligence should be examined, and there is a need for additional working groups, like a Threat Finance Technology Working Group (TFTWG).

Organizational Structure. The second recommendation is to refine the current threat finance organizational structure within DoD.[143]

The proposed organizational structure facilitates integration, collaboration, enhanced utilization of resources, flexibility, and synchronization of effort between DoD and the IA from the tactical to strategic level, and it helps to create one DoD voice at the strategic level. The proposed threat finance organizational and command structure contains four key concepts:

a. Does not change the current command and control relationship between GCCs and CSAs with the Secretary of Defense.

b. Clarifies the synchronization role conducted by USSOCOM.

c. Provides a linkage for maximizing DoD threat finance integration between GCCs and CSAs and the IA through the use of TFEUs.

d. Establishes a mechanism for the DoD to speak with one voice to the IA at the national level.

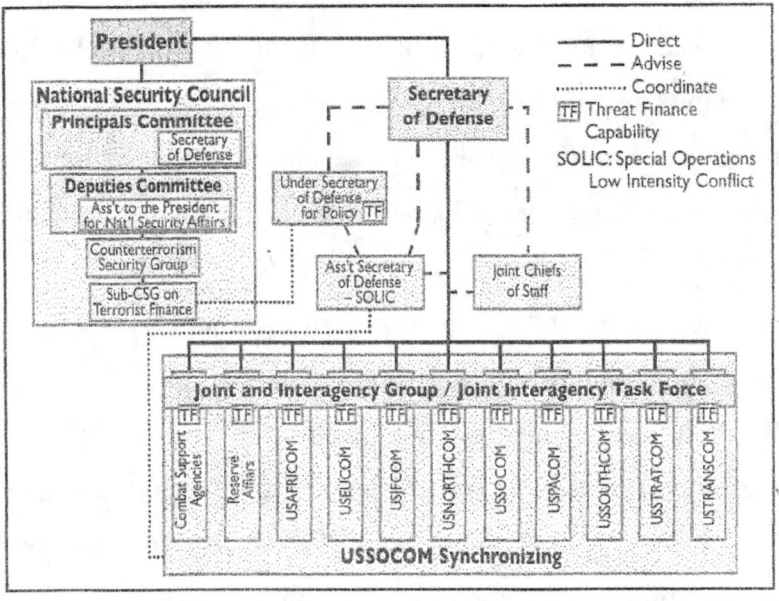

Figure 3. Proposed DoD Threat Finance Organizational and Command Structure

The advantage of the proposed recommendation is that it maximizes the ability of unified combatant commanders to execute their missions and leverage IA capabilities, and vice versa, while synchronizing their efforts across the globe. In addition, it provides a flexible mechanism for DoD to integrate, support, and build relationships with the IA, law enforcement, private sector, allies, and partner nations. Third, it places a threat finance exploitation capability within all the unified commands that can be utilized to disrupt threat finances.

Action list. The third recommendation is that DoD develop a comprehensive and integrated list of actions that could be conducted in support of other government agencies, law enforcement, allies, and partner nations. Some of the actions that DoD could take include:

a. Expanding the definition of threat finance to include economic warfare

b. Providing intelligence collection support along with analysis and the widest dissemination of the information on a *need to share* basis

c. Providing situational awareness through the presence of service members on the ground

d. Providing the conditions that allow the IA, law enforcement, allies, and partner nations to conduct operations within a non- or semi-permissive environment

e. Creating a multilateral information sharing network as discussed earlier in this chapter to facilitate the rapid dissemination and exploitation of information

f. Providing LNOs and increasing interagency and intergovernmental assignments to help break down organizational stovepipes and advance the exchange of ideas and practices for a more effective counterterrorism effort

g. Placing DoD personnel on DoS-lead Financial Systems Assessment Team (FSAT)

h. Infusing and sewing the seeds of doubt, distrust, and deception into terrorist organizations and networks to expand the threat seams and gaps that currently exist

i. Conducting senior leader visits to the various IA

j. Developing a global engagement strategy that integrates 1206 funding

k. Enhancing Sensitive Sight Exploitation (SSE) to improve evidence collection, prosecution, and data collection

l. Creating a data and trend analysis repository that is facilitated by the multilateral information sharing network on a *need to share* basis

m. Expanding computer network exploitation

n. Enhancing capabilities and actions during the initial detention facility screening process which would allow the IA to maximize their resources.

Personnel. The fourth recommendation is to expand education, training, and personnel utilization in the area of threat finance. To accomplish this, DoD should:

a. Establish or integrate a DoD threat finance course at the resident and nonresident level.

b. Send select personnel to the various IA threat finance courses and seminars.

c. Allocate five to seven graduate level threat finance-associated slots a year under the advanced civil schooling program.

d. Develop and integrate threat finance into existing joint doctrine.

e. Establish and promulgate tactics, techniques, and procedures.

f. Promote integration of threat finance during mission readiness exercises, such as those conducted at USJFCOM.

g. Develop a "train the trainer" program.

h. Establish mobile training teams.

i. Host an annual threat finance conference that includes IA, law enforcement, private sector, allies, and partner nations.

j. Identify and track personnel who have been trained in threat finance by creating an enlisted and officer threat finance skill identifier to assist in future threat finance assignment utilization. By developing and fostering subject matter experts through education, training, and personnel utilization, the DoD will be better equipped to disrupt threat finance in a proactive and flexible manner.

Desired Effect

A well thought-out policy and way ahead that is flexible and will facilitate an integrated DoD threat finance effort regarding the IA, law enforcement, private sector, allies, and partner nations. Like any organization, DoD cannot hope to reach its desired end state without first determining what that end state looks like, developing a phased plan to reach that end state, determining alignment of resources, and then developing a policy to facilitate its way ahead.

CONCLUSION

In the years since 9/11, the fight against terrorist organizations has been fought on many fronts, with a great amount of attention being paid to DoD actions in Afghanistan and Iraq and to the prosecutions and preventive measures taken by the DoJ and DHS. Meanwhile, a somewhat quieter, complex campaign against terrorist financing has shown that financial information and intelligence, investigations, prosecutions, sanctions, and diplomacy, when carefully coordinated and facilitated through international standards among the IA, private sector, allies, and partner nations, can make a meaningful contribution to enhance U.S. security, disrupt terrorist operations and mitigate terrorist effects on U.S. strategic interests.[144]

The struggle against terrorism should focus on disrupting terrorist organizations and networks by constricting their operating environment, making it harder for terrorists to conduct operational, logistical, and financial activities. Although it may be impossible to completely eradicate terrorism, it is possible to constrict the operating environment to the extent that it will eventually lead to the suffocation of an individual terrorist organization. For instance, the Abu Nidal organization in the 1980s was the Al Qaeda of today; however, it no longer exists. So too will come a day when the primary international terrorist threat to U.S. interests is no longer posed by Al Qaeda. Sadly, as long as there are intolerant and violent humans on this earth, there will always be another terrorist organization standing in the wings to take its place.[145]

Therefore, if the U.S. hopes to be successful in its efforts against terrorist organizations, it must focus its efforts towards constricting the terrorists' operating environment by:

a. Increasing its expertise and allocation of resources against the disruption of terrorist financing

b. Building capacity for improved governance by working with allies and partner nations across all elements of national power to improve their ability to detect and disrupt terrorist organizations

c. Conducting an integrated and coordinated effort at the international level through: i) the promotion of international intelligence and information sharing; ii) the establishment of common standards, tools, and protocols; and iii) fostering an environment of mutual understanding and respect between U.S. allies and partner nations.

ENDNOTES

1. John Roth, Douglas Greenburg, and Serena Wille, National Commission on Terrorist Attacks Upon the United States, *Monograph on Terrorist Financing: Staff Report to the Commission* (Washington, DC: Government Printing Office, 2004), 17.

2. U.S. Senate, Committee on Banking, Housing, and Urban Affairs, Subcommittee on International Trade and Finance, Testimony by Matthew Levitt, Senior Fellow, Washington Institute for Near East Policy, "Role of Charities and NGOs in the Financing of Terrorist Activities," 1 August 2002, 2, available from http://banking.senate.gov/02_08hrg/080102/ levitt.htm (accessed 18 September 2006).

3. Matthew Levitt, "Untangling the Terror Web: Identifying and Counteracting the Phenomenon of Crossover between Terrorist Groups," *SAIS Review* 24, no. 1 (2004): 33.

4. Roth, et al., 19.

5. The White House, Executive Order 13224, *Blocking Property and Prohibiting Transactions With Persons Who Commit, Threaten to Commit, or Support Terrorism,* 23 September 2001, available from www.fas.org/ irp/offdocs/eo/eo-13224.htm (accessed 27 February 2007).

6. Government Accountability Office, GAO-06-19, Terrorist Financing: Better Strategic Planning Needed to Coordinate U.S. Efforts to Deliver Counterterrorism Financing Training and Technical Assistance Abroad (Washington, DC: GAO, 2005), i.

7. The White House, Executive Order 13224.

8. Section (section) 6(j) of the Export Administration Act, section 40 of the Arms Export Control Act, and section 620A of the Foreign Assistance Act; Pursuant to 8 United States Code (USC) section 1189; Pursuant to 50 USC, section 1701-1706, International Emergency Economic Powers Act (IEEPA); See State Sponsors of Terror, FTOs, SDGTs,

Terrorist Exclusion List, and Specially Designated Nationals, at the U.S. Department of State Web site, available from www.state.gov/, and the U.S. Treasury Department Web site, available from www.ustreas.gov/ (accessed 18 September 2006) and U.S. Laws, Federal Regulations, Federal Register Notices, Cornell School of Law Web site, available from www4.law.cornell.edu/ (accessed 18 September 2006).

9. National Strategy for Combating Terrorism, September 2006, 5.

10. United Nations, *UN Action to Counterterrorism*, 9 December 1999, available from www.un.org/terrorism/ (accessed 27 February 2007).

11. House of Representatives, Committee of Financial Services, Subcommittee on Oversight and Investigations, Statement by Juan C. Zarate, "Patriot Act oversight: Investigating Patters of Terrorist Financing," 12 February 2002, 7, available from financialservices.house.gov/media/ pdf/107-53.pdf (accessed 27 February 2007).

12. General Accounting Office, GAO-04-163, *Terrorist Financing: U.S. Agencies Should Systematically Assess Terrorists' Use of Alternative Financing Mechanisms* (Washington, DC: GAO, 2003), 9-10; and General Accounting Office, GAO-04-501T, *Combating Terrorism, Federal Agencies Face Continuing Challenges in Addressing Terrorist Financing and Money Laundering* (Washington, DC: GAO, 2004), 6.

13. U.S. Senate, Committee on Governmental Affairs, Testimony by Lee L. Wolosky, Schiller Boies, and LLP Flexner, "Terrorist Financing," 29 September 2004, 1-2.

14. Department of the Treasury, Office of Foreign Assets Control, *Terrorist Assets Report 2001*, (Washington, DC: Government Printing Office, December 2001), 9.

15. Roth et al., 29.

16. Ibid., 9.

17. Ibid., 17.

18. U.S. Senate, Committee on Banking, Housing, and Urban Affairs, Testimony of Anthony E. Wayne, Assistant Secretary for Economic and Business Affairs, "The State Department Role in Combating the Financing of Terrorism," 4 April 2006, available from www.state.gov/e/eeb/ rls/rm/2006/ 64109.htm (accessed 18 September 2006) and authors personal analysis.

19. Government Accountability Office, GAO-06-19, 5.

20. Ibid.

21. Richard Shelby, U.S. Senator, Senate Banking Committee to Hold Hearing on Terrorist Financing, Washington, DC: 20. October 2003, 37, available from http://shelby.senate.gov/legislation/legis-record. cfm?id=213770 (accessed 27 February 2007).

22. Government Accountability Office, GAO-06-19, 5.

23. Kitfield and Levey, 2.

24. House of Representatives, Committee on Government Reform, Subcommittee on Criminal Justice Drug Policy and Human Resources, Testimony of Daniel L. Glaser, Director, Executive Office for Terrorist Financing and Financial Crime, U.S. Department of the Treasury, 11 May 2004, 2, available from www.ustreas.gov/press/releases/js1539. htm (accessed 18 September 2006).

25. Headquarters Department of Defense, Joint Publication 1-02, *DoD Dictionary of Military and Associated Terms* (Washington, DC: Government Printing Office, 2006), 146.

26. A More Secured World: Our Shared Responsibility, United Nations, December 2004.

27. National Commission on Terrorist Attacks Against the United States. 22 July 2004; 108-214.

28. Joint Publication 1-02, 375.

29. U.S. Senate, Judiciary Subcommittee on Terrorism, Technology, and Homeland Security, Matthew A. Levitt, Senior Fellow in Terrorism Studies and The Washington Institute for Near East Policy "Terrorist Financing," 10 September 2003, 3.

30. Ibid., 1-3.

31. Ibid., 3.

32. Lee H. Hamilton, Vice Chair, and The National Commission On Terrorist Attacks Upon The United States, "Terrorist Financing," FDCH Congressional Testimony, 1.

33. Roth et al., 17-19.

34. Kitfield and Levey, 2.

35. Lee H. Hamilton, Vice Chair, and The National Commission On Terrorist Attacks Upon The United States, "Terrorist Financing," FDCH Congressional Testimony, 4.

36. The White House, Executive Order 13224.

37. Department of Treasury, Office of Foreign Assets Control, *Terrorist Assets Report 2005.* Fourteen Report to Congress on Assets in the United States of Terrorist Countries and Internal Terrorism Program Designees, December 2005, 5, available from www.treas.gov/offices/enforcement/ofac/reports/tar2005.pdf (accessed 18 September 2006).

38. Roth et al., 1.

39. Government Accountability Office, GAO-06-19, 2.

40. Ibid., 3.

41. Ibid., 33.

42. Department of Treasury, *Terrorist Assets Report 2005*, 6.

43. Ibid.

44. Government Accountability Office, GAO-06-19, 33.

45. U.S. Senate, Committee on Governmental Affairs, Testimony by Lee L. Wolosky, Schiller Boies, and LLP Flexner, "Terrorist Financing," 29 September 2004, 3.

46. Todd M. Hinnen, "The Cyber-Front in the War on Terrorism: Curbing Terrorist use of the Internet," *The Columbia Science and Technology Law Review*, vol. 5 (2004): 2.

47. As referenced in Appendix C.

48. General Accounting Office, GAO-04-501T, 6.

49. See Appendix D.

50. General Accounting Office, GAO-04-163, 3.

51. See Figure 1: Example Terrorist Organization Hierarchal Structure; and Levitt, "Terrorist Financing," 19.

52. See Figure 2; and John Arquilla and David Ronfeldt, *Networks and Netwars: The Future of Terror, Crime, and Military* (Santa Monica CA: National Defense Research Institute, 2001), 30.

53. Levitt, "Terrorist Financing," 19.

54. Levitt, *SAIS Review*, 2.

55. Levitt, "Terrorist Financing," 1-3.

56. Joint Publication 1-02, 101.

57. White House, "National Strategy for Combating Terrorism," September 2006, 17. available from www.state.gov/s/ct/rls/wh/71803.htm (accessed 15 March 2007).

58. Arquilla and Ronfeldt, 33.

59. Ibid., 34.

60. For the purposes of this monograph, the term *Internet* does not include the separate network infrastructures provided for automated teller machine (ATM), wire transfer, or debit and credit card networks, although it does include Web-based applications through which debit, credit or value card transactions may be accomplished.

61. White House, "National Strategy for Combating Terrorism," 17.

62. White House, "National Strategy for Combating Terrorism," 12.

63. Courtney J. Linn, "How Terrorists Exploit Gaps in U.S. Anti-Money Laundering Laws to Secrete Plunder," *Journal of Money Laundering Control* 8, no. 3 (March 2005): 1.

64. The White House, *National Security Strategy of the United States of America* (Washington, DC: Government Printing Office, 2006), 9-45.

65. Raphael Perl, *Terrorism and National Security: Issues and Trends* (Washington, DC: Congressional Research Service, The Library of Congress, 2004), 14-15, available from www.fas.org/irp/crs/IB10119.pdf (accessed 27 February 2007).

66. See Appendix D for a more in-depth description of the various organizations mentioned in this section.

67. Government Accountability Office, GAO-06-19, 2-6.

68. See Appendix D for further information and discussion.

69. Perl, 14-15. Authors note: It is important to understand that the NSC does not control the law enforcement community or its actions, it merely maintains coordination authority.

70. See Appendix D.

71. PDD 39, June 1995, 1.

72. General Accounting Office, GAO-03-165, *Combating Terrorism: Interagency Framework and Agency Programs to Address the Overseas Threat* (Washington, DC: GAO, 2003), 147.

73. See Appendix D for more detailed information, composition and discussion on the TFI.

74. See Appendix D for a more detailed list of Treasury offices, services, task forces and networks.

75. U.S. Senate, Committee on Banking, Housing, and Urban Affairs, Testimony of Anthony E. Wayne, Assistant Secretary for Economic and Business Affairs, "The State Department Role in Combating the Financing of Terrorism," 4 April 2006, 3, available from www.state. gov/e/eeb/rls/rm/2006/ 64109.htm (accessed 18 September 2006).

76. General Accounting Office, GAO-03-165, 150.

77. See Appendix D for a more detailed list of DoS agencies, bureaus, councils, and offices.

78. Barry Sabin, Acting Deputy Assistant Attorney General, and Department of Justice, *"Counterterrorism Financing,"* FDCH Congressional Testimony, 2006, 1-2.

79. Government Accounting Office, GAO-03-165, 149.

80. See Appendix D for a more detailed list of DoJ bureaus, administrations, sections, branches, task forces, and offices.

81. Government Accounting Office, GAO-03-165, 149.

82. See Appendix D for a more detailed list of DHS units and bureaus.

83. House Armed Services Committee, Subcommittee on Terrorism, Unconventional Threats, and Capabilites and House Financial Services, Subcommittee on Oversight and

Investigations, Statement of James Q. Roberts, "Terrorist and Insurgent Financing," 28 July 2005, 2, available from www.dod.   mil/dodgc/olc/docs/Test05-07-28Roberts.doc (accessed 18 September 2006).

84. CW3 Thomas Newell, *The Use of Special Operations Forces in Combating Terrorist Finances,"* Naval Post Graduate School, Monterey California, 2006, i.

85. House Armed Services Committee, Subcommittee on Terrorism, Unconventional Threats and Capabilities, Statement by Marshall Billingslea, "Special Operations Forces Acquisition," 1 April 2003, available from www.globalsecurity.org/military/library/congress/2003_hr/03-04- 01billingslea.htm (accessed 18 September 2006).

86. Thomas O'Connell, *"Update On Special Operations Forces,"* 2004, Testimony before The Senate Committee On Armed Services, United States Senate, 6-7.

87. House Armed Services Committee, "Terrorist and Insurgent Financing," 3-4.

88. Thomas W. O'Connell, *Defense Perspectives: The War on Terrorism,* 2006, 16-17, available from www.dtic.mil/ndia/2006solic/oconnell. pdf (accessed 18 September 2006).

89. Jimmy Gurule, "The Global Effort to Stop Terrorist Financing," *Hampton Roads International Security Quarterly* (January 2004): 2.

90. Department of the Treasury, Fact sheet, *Contributions by the Department of Treasury to the Financial War on Terror,* September 2002, 5, available from www.ustreas.gov/press/releases/ reports/2002910184556291211. pdf (accessed 18 September 2006).

91. See Appendix E: International Organizations and Efforts to Disrupt Terrorist Financing for a more comprehensive list of these organizations and efforts.

92. Todd M. Hinnen, Chief Counsel of the Senate Judiciary Committee, Annotated comment on draft version 1.1 of this monograph, 3 March 2007.

93. United Nations, *Coordinating Counterterrorism Actions Within and Beyond the UN system*, available from www.un.org/terrorism/cttaskforce.html (accessed 27 February 2007).

94. United Nations, *United Nations Action to Counterterrorism*, available from www.un.org/terrorism/ (accessed 27 February 2007).

95. See Appendix E: International Organizations and Efforts to Disrupt Terrorist Financing for a more complete description of United Nations efforts.

96. Gurulé, 3-4.

97. See Appendix E: International Organizations and Efforts to Disrupt Terrorist Financing for a description of FATF Forty Recommendations on Money Laundering and Nine Special Recommendations on Terrorist Financing.

98. Financial Action Task Force, *Report on Money Laundering and Typologies 2002-2003*. 14 February 2003, 1, available from www.pszaf.hu/ resource.aspx?ResourceID= penzmos_fatf_ty2003 (accessed 18 September 2006).

99. House of Representatives, Financial Services, Subcommittee on Oversight and Investigations and the House of Representatives, International Relations, Subcommittee on International Terrorism and Nonproliferation; Testimony of Stuart Levey, Under Secretary, and Department of the Treasury, "Terror Financing in the Middle East; Terror Financing in the Middle East," 4 May 2005, 3, available from www.treas.gov/press/ releases/js2427.htm (accessed 18 September 2006).

100. Government Accounting Office, GAO-03-165, 152.

101. Ibid., 141-142.

102. The International Criminal Police Organization, *Financial and High-Tech Crimes,* available from

www.interpol.int/Public/FinancialCrime/ Default.asp (accessed 27 February 2007).

103. The International Criminal Police Organization, *Fusion Task Force,* available from www.interpol.int/Public/FusionTaskForce/default.asp (accessed 27 February 2007).

104. Department of State, *U.S. Interagency Efforts to Combat Terrorist Financing*, available from www.state.gov/e/eb/rls/rm/2003/29144. htm (accessed 18 September 2006).

105. United Nations, *UN Action to Counterterrorism*, 1.

106. Summary of all 13 conventions available from http://untreaty.un.org/ English/Terrorism.asp.

107. United Nations, *International Convention for the Suppression of the Financing of Terrorism*, 1999, 1-15, available from www.un.org/law/ cod/finterr.htm (accessed 18 September 2006).

108. United Nations, *Convention against Transnational Organized Crime*, 2000, 1, available from www.unodc.org/adhoc/palermo/convmain. html (accessed 18 September 2006).

109. United Nations, *United Nations Convention against Transnational Organized Crime*, 2000, 1-34, available from www.unodc.org/unodc/en/ crime_cicp_convention.html (accessed 27 February 2007).

110. Government Accounting Office, GAO-06-19, 8.

111. House of Representatives, Committee on Government Reforms, Subcommittee on Technology and Information Policy Intergovernmental Relations and the Census, Testimony of George Glass, Director of the Office of Terrorism Finance and Sanctions Policy, Department of State, "U.S. Interagency Efforts to Combat Terrorist Financing," 15 December 2003, 3, available from www.globalsecurity.org/ security/library/ congress/2003_h/031215-state_testimony.pdf (accessed 18 September 2006).

112. United Nations Security Council, *Resolution 1267*, 15 October 1999, 1-4, available from www.un.org/Docs/scres/1999/sc99.htm (accessed 1 March 2007).

113. The White House, Executive Order 13224, 1.

114. United Nations Security Council, *Resolution 1269*, 19 October 1999, 1-2, available from www.un.org/Docs/scres/1999/sc99.htm (accessed 1 March 2007).

115. United Nations Security Council, *Resolution 1373*, 28 September 2001, 1-4, available from www.un.org/docs/scres/2001/sc2001.htm (accessed 1 March 2007).

116. United Nations Security Council, *Resolution 1617*, 29 July 2005, 1-8, available from www.un.org/Docs/sc/unsc_resolutions05.htm (accessed 1 March 2007).

117. United Nations Security Council, *Resolution 1730*, 19 December 2006, available from www.un.org/Docs/sc/unsc_resolutions06.htm (accessed 1 March 2007).

118. United Nations Security Council, *Resolution 1735*, 22 December 2006, available from www.un.org/Docs/sc/unsc_resolutions06.htm (accessed 1 March 2007).

119. See Appendix D for a more in depth list that pertain to terrorist financing.

120. 85th Congress of the U.S. 1977, *International Emergency Economic Powers Act*, available from www.law.cornell.edu/uscode/50/usc_ sup_01_50_10_35.html (accessed 18 March 2006).

121. Ibid., 5.

122. Charles Doyle, *Antiterrorism and Effective Death Penalty Act of 1996: A Summary*, 3 June 1996, available from www.fas.org/irp/crs/96-499. htm (accessed 18 September 2006).

123. 104th Congress of the U.S. 1996, *Antiterrorism and Effective Death Penalty Act,* 1-150, available from usinfo.state.gov/usa/infousa/laws/ majorlaw/s735.htm (accessed 18 September 2006).

124. Ibid., 50-55.

125. House of Representatives, Committee on International Relations, Testimony of Herbert A. Biern, "The Bank Secrecy Act and the USA Patriot Act," 17 November 2004, available from www.federalreserve.gov/boarddocs/testimony/2004/20041117/ default.htm (accessed 18 September 2006).

126. Department of the Treasury, *Bank Secrecy Act*, 1970, available from www.fincen.gov/reg_statutes.html (accessed 18 September 2006).

127. Scott Sulzer, "Money Laundering: The Scope of the Problem and Attempts to Combat It," *Tennessee Law Review*, 143 (1995): 153.

128. *Uniting and Strengthening America by Providing Appropriate Tools Required to Intercept and Obstruct Terrorism Acts of 2001*, Pub. L. No. 107-56, 115 stat. 272 (codified and amended in scattered sections of 8, 15, 18, 22, 31, 42, 49, and 50 of the United States Code), available from www.fincen.gov/pa_main.html (accessed 18 September 2006).

129. House of Representatives, Committee on Government Reform, Subcommittee on Criminal Justice Drug Policy and Human Resources, Testimony of Daniel L. Glaser, Director, Executive Office for Terrorist Financing and Financial Crime, U.S. Department of the Treasury, 11 May 2004, 1, available from www.ustreas.gov/press/releases/js1539. htm (accessed 18 September 2006).

130. EO 13224 gives the Departments of the Treasury and State the ability to designate terrorists and terrorist financiers and gives the Treasury Department the ability to implement orders that freeze the assets of designated terrorists.

131. The White House, Executive Order 13224, 1.

132. Department of Treasury, *Terrorist Assets Report 2005*, 1-6.

133. The White House, *The National Security Council*, available from www. whitehouse.gov/nsc/ (accessed 27 February 2007).

134. National Counterterrorism Center, *NCTC*, available from www.nctc.gov/ (accessed 18 September 2007).

135. U.S. Senate, Committee on Banking, Housing and Urban Affairs, Testimony of John S. Pistole, Assistant Director, Counterterrorism Division, FBI, "Identifying, Tracking and Dismantling the Financial Structure of Terrorist Organizations," 25 September 2003, 5, available from www. fbi.gov/ congress/congress03/pistole092503.htm (accessed 11 March 2007).

136. Levitt, "Terrorist Financing," 35.

137. The White House, Executive Order 13356, *Strengthening the Sharing of Terrorism Information to Protect Americans*, 27 August 2004, available from www.fas.org/irp/offdocs/eo/eo-13356.htm (accessed 27 February 2007).

138. National Counterterrorism Center, *NCTC and Information Sharing, Five Years Since 9/11: A Progress Report* (Washington, DC: GAO, 2006), 10, available from www.nctc.gov/docs/report_card_final.pdf (accessed 28 September 2006).

139. Such systems include:
    a. NCTC Online (NOL)
    b. Joint Worldwide Intelligence Communications System (JWICS)
    c. Law Enforcement Online (LEO)
    d. FinCEN Communications Network
    e. GRIFFIN
    f. FBI Intranet
    g Data Analysis and Research for Trade Transparency System (DARTTS)
    h Secret Internet Protocol Router Network (SIPRNet)
    i. DoD Intelligence Information System (DODIIS)
    j. INTERPOL's I-24/7 Global Police Communications System

k. Egmont Group Secure Web.

140. See Appendix F, Worldwide Information and Intelligence Network (WIIN), for design and capabilities of proposed system.

141. Department of Defense, *National Military Strategic Plan for the War on Terrorism*, 1 February 2006, available from www.defenselink.mil/qdr/ docs/2005-01-25-Strategic-Plan.pdf (accessed 18 September 2006).

142. The current unified commands are Reserve Affairs Worldwide Support, USEUCOM, USJFCOM, USNORTHCOM, USPACOM, USSOUTHCOM, USSOCOM, USSTRATCOM, USTRANSCOM.

143. See Figure 3, Proposed DoD Threat Finance Organizational Structure

144. Joseph M. Myers, "The Silent Struggle against Terrorist Financing," *Georgetown Journal of International Affairs* 6, no. 1 (Winter 2005): 33.

145. Levitt, "Terrorist Financing," 3.

APPENDIX A-FTO Locations and the Original Pan-Islamic Caliphate

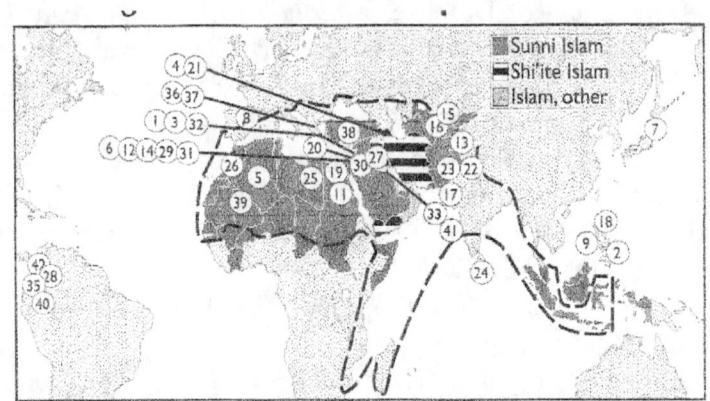

1. Abu Nidal Organization (ANO)	24. Liberation Tigers of Tamil Eelam (LTTE)
2. Abu Sayyaf Group (ASG)	25. Libtan Islamic Fighting Group (LIFG)
3. Al-Aqsa Martyrs Brigade	26. Moroccan Islamic Combatant Group
4. Ansar al-Islam	(LIFG)
5. Armed Islamic Group (GIA)	27. Mujahidin-e Khalq Organization (MEK)
6. Asbat al-Anser	28. National Liberation Army (ELN)
7. Aum Shinrikyo	29. Palestine Liberation Front (PLF)
8. Basque Fatherland and Liberty (ETA)	30. Palestinian Islamic Jihad (PIJ)
9. Communist Party of the Phillipines /New People's Army	31. Popular Front for the Liberation of Palestine (PFLP)
10. Continuity Irish Republican Army	32. PFLP-General Command (PFLP-GC)
11. Gama's al-Islamiyya (Islamic Group)	33. Al Qaida
12. HAMAS (Islamic Resistance Movement)	34. Real IRA (RIRA)
13. Harakat ul-Mujahidin (HUM)	35. Revolutionary Armed Forces of Columbia (FARC)
14. Hizballah (Party of God)	36. Revolutionary Nuclei (formerly ELA)
15. Islamic Jihad Group	37. Revolutionary Organization 17 November (17 November)
16. Islamic Movement of Uzbekistan (IMU)	38. Revolutionary People's Liberation Party/ Front (DHKP/C)
17. Jaish-e-Mohammed (JEM) (Army of Mohammed)	39. Salafist Group for Call and Combat (GSPC)
18. Jemaah Islamiya organization (JI)	40. Shining Path (Sendero Luminoso, SL)
19. al-Jihad (Egyptian Islamic Jihad)	41. Tarzim Qa'idat al-Jihad fi Bilad al-Rafidayn (QJBR)
20. Kahane Chai (Kach)	42. United Self-Defense Forces of Columbia (AUC)
21. Kongra-Gel (KGK, formerly PKK, KADEK)	
22. Lashkar-e Tayyiba (LT) (Army of the Righteous)	
23. Lashkar i Jhangvi (LJ)	

Figure A-1. The approximate location of the 42 FTOs, the original Pan-Islamic Caliphate, and the distribution of the types of Islam.[1]

1. Adapted and integrated by the author from:
   a.   Wikipedia,
   http://de.wikipedia.org/wiki/Bild:Weltreligionen.png
   (accessed 18 September 2006)
   b. U.S. Department of State, Foreign Terrorist
   Organizations,   11   October   2005,
   www.state.gov/s/ct/rls/fs/37191.htm   (accessed   18
   September 2006)
   c. Office of the Coordinator for Counterterrorism,
   www.state.gov/s/ ct/ (accessed 18 September 2006).

APPENDIX B. Alternative Financing Mechanisms

Table B-1. Examples of Alternative Financing
Mechanisms: Sources, Movement, and Storage[1]

Alternative Financing Mechanisms	Sources	Movement	Storage
Criminal Activity			
Credit Card Fraud	X		
Counterfeiting			
Extortion	X		
Identity Theft	X		
Immigration Benefit Fraud	X		
Intellectual Property Piracy	X		
Kidnapping for Ransom	X		
Welfare Benefit Fraud	X		
Currency			
Debit or Stored Value "Smart" Cards		X	X
Digital Currency		X	X
Money		X	X
Phone Value Cards		X	X
Travelers Checks		X	X
Systems			
Alternative Remittance "Informal Value Transfer"		X	
Hawala		X	
Hundi		X	
Cash Couriers		X	
Charities	X	X	
Corporate Contributors	X	X	
Financial Facilitators		X	
Formal Banking		X	X
Individual Contributors, Witting & Unwitting	X		
Internet	X	X	X
Auctions	X	X	
Casinos	X	X	X
Islamic Banks		X	X
Not for Profit Organizations, Witting & Unwitting	X	X	
State Sponsors	X	X	X
Trade Based	X	X	
Unlicensed Money Services Businesses		X	
Wire Transfers		X	
Trade in Commodities			
Contraband Cigarettes	X		
Counterfeit Goods	X		
Diamonds	X	X	X
Drug Trafficking	X		
Gemstones	X	X	X
Gold	X	X	X
Weapons	X		

Adapted by the author from *Terrorist Financing: U.S. Agencies Should Systematically Assess Terrorists' Use of Alternative Financing Mechanisms*, GAO-04-163, 2003, and the authors analysis based on government, industry, and various other research sources.

APPENDIX C: U.S. Organizations and Efforts to Disrupt Terrorist Financing

Major USG departments and agencies, including their major bureaus, divisions, and offices, with descriptions of their efforts. (Adapted from the "Terrorist Financing: Better Strategic Planning Needed to Coordinate U.S. Efforts to Deliver Counterterrorism Financing Training and Technical Assistance Abroad: GAO-06-19," 2005, GAO Reports 1, 39-43.)

1. National Security Council (NSC)

The National Security Act of 1947, as amended, established the National Security Council to advise the President of the U.S. with respect to the integration of domestic, foreign, and military policies relating to national security. In short, the NSC advises the President on national security and foreign policy; serves as a forum for discussion among the President, presidential advisers, and cabinet officials; and is the President's mechanism for coordinating policy among government agencies on interdisciplinary issues. The NSC is responsible for the overall coordination of the interagency framework for combating terrorism including the financing of terrorist operations. Under the NSC structure are a series of committees and working groups which address terrorism issues.

1.1. **Counterterrorism Security Group (CSG).** The CSG is chaired by the NSC which is composed of high level representatives (at the Assistant Secretary level) from key federal agencies (DHS, FBI, CIA, DoD, DHS, DoJ, Treasury Department, NCTC as well as representatives of other departments or agencies as needed). The purpose of the CSG is to share information and coordinate counterterrorism action on a daily basis against threats to U.S. interests domestically and abroad. A series of interagency working groups under the CSG coordinate specific efforts as needed.

1.2. Sub-CSG on Terrorist Finance. The President established a Sub-CSG under the auspices of the NSC to ensure the proper coordination of counterterrorism financing activities and information sharing among all agencies including the Central Intelligence Agency, Department of Defense, Department of Justice, Department of Homeland Security, National Security Council, State Department, and Treasury Department, as well as the law enforcement community. Chaired by the Treasury Department, Office of the General Counsel. The Sub-CSG on Terrorist Financing was formalized at the end of 2005. The SubCSG coordinates the development and implementation of policies to combat terrorist financing and provides analysis on these issues. The Sub-CSG generally meets at least once a month to coordinate the USG's campaign against terrorist financing. The meetings generally focus on ensuring that all relevant components of the federal government are acting in a coordinated and effective manner to combat terrorist financing.

1.2. Directorate for Combating Terrorism. The Directorate for Combating Terrorism, which is part of NSC, is headed by the National Coordinator at the Deputy National Security Advisor level. The National Coordinator will work within the National Security Council, report to the President through the Assistant to the President for National Security Affairs, and produce for him an annual Security Preparedness Report. The National Coordinator will also provide advice regarding budgets for counterterror programs and lead in the development of guidelines that might be needed for crisis management.

2. Treasury Department

Since PDD 39 in June 1995, the Secretary of the Treasury has been responsible for identifying and blocking terrorist financing. These efforts were stepped up after the terrorist attacks of 9/11, when the President signed Executive Order 13224.Treasury also has the responsibility to protect the integrity of the financial system by administering the Bank Secrecy Act (BSA), as enhanced by Title III of the USA Patriot Act.

2.1. Office of Terrorism and Financial Intelligence (TFI), Treasury Department. TFI marshals the department's intelligence and enforcement functions with the twin aims of safeguarding the financial system against illicit use and combating rogue nations, terrorist facilitators, money launderers, drug kingpins, and other national security threats. TFI also brings together Treasury's intelligence, regulatory, law enforcement, sanctions, and policy components. TFI allows Treasury to:

a. Better develop and target their intelligence analysis and financial data to detect how terrorists are exploiting financial systems and to design methods to stop them and their financial infrastructure.

b. Better coordinate aggressive law, sanctions and regulatory enforcement programs, while working with other components of the government and the private sector.

c. Continue to develop a strong international coalition required to combat terrorist financing, in part by facilitating the development and exchange of financial information that supports their requests for collaborative action.

d. Ensure accountability, thus helping to achieve better results.

2.1.1. Office of Terrorist Financing, TFI, Treasury Department. TFI develops, organizes, and implements USG strategies to combat terrorist financing and financial crime, both internationally and domestically. Is the policy and outreach apparatus for the Treasury Department on the issues of terrorist financing, money laundering, financial crime, and sanctions. Provides increased coordination with other elements of the USG, including law enforcement and regulatory agencies.

Domestically, the office is charged with continuing to develop and implement the USG's national money laundering strategy as well as other policies and programs. Serves as a primary outreach body to the private sector and other stakeholders.

2.1.1.1. The Office of Terrorist Finance and Financial Crimes (TFFC), Office of Terrorist Financing, TFI, Treasury Department.

TFFC, formerly the Executive Office of Terrorist Finance and Financial Crime (EOTF/FC), was created in March 2003 and assumed the main functions of the former Office of Enforcement. TFFC became part of TFI under the Office of Terrorist Financing in August 2004. The office is charged with coordinating Treasury Department's efforts to combat terrorist financing both in the U.S. and abroad. Participates in U.S. interagency assessments of countries' capabilities to combat terrorist financing and money laundering. Provides technical advice and practical guidance on how international standards for combating money laundering and terrorist financing should be adopted and implemented. Develops U.S. strategies and policies to deter terrorist financing, domestically and internationally. Develops and implements the National Money Laundering Strategy as well as other policies and programs to prevent financial crimes.

2.1.2. Office of Intelligence and Analysis (OIA), TFI, Treasury Department.

The overall purpose of OIA is to ensure that the Treasury Department properly analyzes relevant intelligence, adding their own unique expertise and capabilities, to create actionable financial intelligence that Treasury and the rest of the USG can use effectively. Priorities include

103

identifying and attacking the financial infrastructure of terrorist groups; assisting in efforts to identify and address vulnerabilities that may be exploited by terrorists and criminals in domestic and international financial systems; and promoting stronger relationships with our partners in the U.S. and around the world.

2.1.3. Office of Foreign Asset Control (OFAC), TFI, Treasury Department.

OFAC acts under Presidential wartime and national emergency powers, as well as under authority granted by specific legislation to administer and enforce economic and trade sanctions based on U.S. foreign policy and national security goals against targeted foreign countries, Foreign Terrorist Organizations (FTOs), terrorists, international narcotics traffickers, and those engaged in activities related to the proliferation of weapons of mass destruction (WMD). In administering and enforcing its economic sanctions programs, OFAC focuses on:

a. Assisting U.S. persons in complying with the sanctions prohibitions through its compliance and licensing efforts

b. Penalizing U.S. persons violating the prohibitions

c. Working with other USG agencies, including law enforcement

d. Coordinating and working with other nations to implement similar strategies.

Since 1995, OFAC has administered three sanctions programs targeting international terrorists and terrorist organizations. OFAC also administers five sanctions programs relating to terrorism-supporting governments and regimes.

2.1.4. Financial Crimes Enforcement Network (FinCEN), TFI, Treasury Department.

FinCEN was created in 1990 to maximize information sharing among law enforcement agencies and its other partners in the regulatory and financial communities. FinCEN works to safeguard the financial system from the abuse of federal crime, including terrorist financing, money laundering, and other illicit activities. FinCEN achieves this mission through its fulfillment of four essential roles:

a. Administering the BSA

b. Supporting law enforcement, intelligence, and regulatory agencies through sharing and analysis of financial intelligence

c. Building global cooperation with counterpart financial intelligence units

d. Networking people, ideas and information.

FinCEN provides financial intelligence training and technical assistance to a broad range of government officials, financial regulators, law enforcement officers, and others abroad with a focus on the creation and improvement of financial intelligence units. FinCEN partners with other governments and international entities to coordinate training and participates in the assessments of foreign governments' financial intelligence capabilities.

2.1.5. The Treasury Executive Office for Asset Forfeiture and Treasury Forfeiture Fund (TEOAF), TFI, Treasury Department. TEOAF administers the Treasury Forfeiture Fund (TFF). The TFF was established in 1992 as the successor to what was then the Customs Forfeiture Fund. It is the receipt account for the deposit of nontax forfeitures made by the following Member Agencies: Internal Revenue Service Criminal Investigation Division (IRS-CI), U.S. Treasury Department; U.S. Immigration and Customs Enforcement (U.S. ICE), Department of Homeland Security (DHS); U.S. Customs and Border Protection (U.S. CBP), DHS; U.S. Secret Service (USSS), DHS; and U.S. Coast Guard, DHS.

2.2. Internal Revenue Service (IRS), Treasury Department. Assists with terrorist finance criminal cases within the U.S. with an emphasis on charitable organizations.

2.2.1. IRS-Criminal Investigation (IRS-CI), IRS, Treasury Department. The IRS-CI Division specializes in analyzing complex financial information and determining whether that information is in violation of tax laws, money laundering laws, and the BSA. In addition, IRS-CI is heavily involved with the Joint Terrorism Task Force (JTTF), Operation Green Quest and similar partnerships focused on disrupting and dismantling terrorist financing. In particular, IRS-CI is focused on preventing the abuse of charities by those who support terrorism. The IRS-CI maintains a direct reporting relationship to the Office of Terrorist Financing.

2.3. **Office of Technical Assistance/Enforcement Policy and Administration Program, Treasury Department.** Provides a range of training and technical assistance including intermittent and long-term resident advisors to senior-level representatives in various ministries and central banks on a range of areas including financial reforms related to money laundering and terrorist financing. Conducts and participates in assessments of foreign government anti-money-laundering regimes for the purpose of developing technical assistance plans.

2.4. **Office of International Affairs, Treasury Department.** The Office of International Affairs works bilaterally and multilaterally to build and maintain the international coalition against terrorist finances along with other federal agencies, including the DoS, DoJ, FBI, and the intelligence community.

2.4.1. **Liaison Officer (LNO), Geographic Combatant Commanders (GCCs), Department of Defense.** Treasury LNOs:
a) identify and propose joint GCC Treasury initiatives;
b) provide "area of responsibility" (AOR) perspective to OFAC and OIA in response to taskings for the development of administrative records for designation of target support networks;
c) communicate theater strategy, plans, initiatives, and analytical findings to Treasury; and

d) provide technical and policy expertise to GCCs, staff, and components on Treasury's authorities, programs and initiatives that relate to GCC objectives within its AOR.

2.4.2. Financial Attachés, Office of International Affairs, Treasury Department. Develop extensive contacts with foreign finance ministries, foreign regulatory authorities, central banks and financial market participants. Financial Attachés explain new U.S. policies to their foreign counterparts. They also collect, report, interpret, and forecast macroeconomic and financial developments and policies in their assigned countries.

3. Department of State (DoS)

The DoS is the lead agency for USG efforts to combat terrorism overseas. Within the department, multiple bureaus and offices manage various programs and activities to combat terrorism abroad. DoS also works with other USG agencies, foreign government agencies, and international organizations in carrying out its counterterrorism programs and activities. As the lead foreign affairs agency, the DoS serves as the statutorily-appointed coordinator and overall clearinghouse for the wide span of counterterrorism activities conducted overseas by the USG. In addition, the Departments of State, Treasury, and Justice work with other countries on a bilateral and multilateral basis to identify and freeze terrorist assets. Offices from other IA's lend their expertise on a bilateral and multilateral basis to provide technical assistance and training to countries to help them meet international standards to combat terrorist financing.

3.1. The Office of the Coordinator for Counterterrorism (S/CT), DoS. In conjunction with International Narcotics and Law Enforcement Affairs, S/CT has the lead in coordinating capacity building to combat terrorist financing in other countries. With the concurrence of the Departments of Justice and Treasury, designates foreign terrorist organizations, individuals, and groups for a variety of purposes, including blocking terrorism-related financing. S/CT also coordinates and funds U.S. training and technical assistance provided by other U.S. agencies to develop or enhance the capacity of a selected countries; manages or provides funding for other counterterrorism financing programs for DoS, other IA, ILEAs, international entities, and regional bodies; leads the U.S. IA assessments of foreign government vulnerabilities; coordinates U.S. counterterrorism policy and efforts with foreign governments to deter terrorist financing; provides funds and policy guidance to the Office of Antiterrorism Assistance Program and determines which countries are authorized to participate in the program; and publishes an unclassified report called Patterns of Global Terrorism.

3.1.1. Counterterrorism Finance Unit, S/CT, DoS. The unit implements significant parts of the U.S. strategy to cut off financial support to terrorists. The unit coordinates the delivery of technical assistance and training to governments around the world that seek to improve their ability to investigate, identify, and interdict the flow of money to terrorist groups. The unit, along with the Bureau of International Narcotics and Law Enforcement, funds and coordinates IA training and technical assistance in the five basic components of a comprehensive counterterrorist financing/anti-money-laundering regime:
a) legal frameworks,
b) financial regulatory systems,
c) financial intelligence units,
d) law enforcement, and
e) judicial/prosecutorial development.

The unit also works with the Office of Terrorist Finance and Economic Sanctions Policy, DoS to foster a coordinated USG response to terrorist financing, the White House, OFAC, the Financial Action Task Force (FATF), and other international organizations and foreign governments to disrupt terrorist finances.

3.2. Bureau of International Narcotics and Law Enforcement Affairs (INL), DoS.

INL has primary responsibility within DoS for international anti-crime issues, including programs to combat money laundering and other financial crimes. In conjunction with S/CT it has the lead in coordinating capacity building to combat terrorist financing in other countries. INL provides funding to the DoJ and Treasury, to assist in the training and assistance of foreign governments to strengthen their financial and regulatory regimes to reduce terrorist financing. These programs are aimed at providing front-line states with technical assistance in drafting antiterrorist financing legislation, and training for bank regulators, investigators, and prosecutors to identify and combat financial crime, particularly terrorist financing.

3.3. Office of Antiterrorism Assistance Program (ATA), Bureau of Diplomatic Security (DS), DoS.

ATA strategy involves applying all aspects of national power in conjunction with U.S. partners and allies to target terrorists' leadership and sanctuaries and to address the conditions terrorists seek to exploit. Since 1983, ATA has provided a key tool for providing partner countries the training, equipment, and technology they need to improve their ability to contribute effectively to these aims by deterring or capturing and prosecuting terrorists and their supporters.

3.3.1. Diplomatic Security Antiterrorism Assistance Programs, ATA, DS, DoS.

The program is run by the ATA, DS and provides law enforcement training for foreign counterparts and, through International Law Enforcement Agencies (ILEAs), to develops the skills necessary to combat terrorism, to include:

a) protecting national borders,

b) protecting critical infrastructure,

c) protecting the national leadership,

d) responding to and resolving terrorist incidents,

e) investigating and prosecuting those responsible for terrorist acts,

f) responding to WMD attacks,

g) managing kidnapping for ransom crimes, and

h) responding to terrorist incidents resulting in mass casualties or fatalities.

The program provides a wide range of courses to strengthen the capacities of recipient countries. The training includes traditional courses such as hostage negotiations, bomb detection, and airport security. In recent years however, ATA has developed new courses for countering terrorism financing and defeating cyber-terrorism. It also has provided a series of seven seminars to help other countries strengthen their counterterrorism legislation.

3.4. The Overseas Security Advisory Council (OSAC), DoS.

OSAC is a Federal Advisory Committee with a USG Charter to promote security cooperation between American business and private sector interests worldwide and the DoS. OSAC helps over 2,800 businesses, universities, religious groups, and nongovernmental organizations cope with security threats by sharing information on crime and terrorism and by providing insight into political, economic, social, and cultural climates around the globe. The objectives of the council as outlined in the charter are:

a. Establish continuing liaison and to provide for operational security cooperation between DoS security functions and the private sector.

b. Provide for regular and timely interchange of information between the private sector and the DoS concerning developments in the overseas security environment.

c. Recommend methods and provide material for coordinating security planning and implementation of security programs

d. Recommend methods to protect the competitiveness of American businesses operating worldwide.

3.5. **Bureau of Economic Energy, and Business Affairs (EEB), DoS.** Maintains the leadership role in the IA effort to combat terrorist financing. Formulates and carries out U.S. foreign economic policy, integrating U.S. economic interests with foreign policy goals so that U.S. firms and investors can compete on an equal basis with their counterparts overseas. In addition, EEB coordinates terrorist financing policy and coalition building on terrorist financing, including related to United Nations sanctions under Resolution 1267, and chairs the Coalition Building meetings, which supports U.S Government efforts to develop strategies and activities to obtain international cooperation.

3.5.1. **The Office of Terrorism Finance and Economic Sanctions Policy (TFS), EEB, DoS.** Is responsible for leading the effort to build international coalition support to block terrorist assets. Coordinates policy implementation at the working level, largely through the network of Terrorism Finance Coordinating Officers located at embassies worldwide as directed by the Energy, Sanctions, and Commodities (ESC). In conjunction with other bureaus and agencies, coordinates efforts to build international support for efforts against terrorist finance. In addition, TFS works through U.S. missions around the world to a) encourage countries to take actions to freeze terrorist assets when found, b) develop new initiatives to strengthen international cooperation against terrorist finance, and c) support efforts to provide technical assistance to foreign governments working against terrorist finance. TFS coordinates efforts to a) create, modify, or terminate unilateral sanctions regimes as appropriate to the changing international situation, such as Iraq and Libya; b) develop strategies for implementation of specific aspects of sanctions regimes; and c) provide foreign policy guidance on specific commercial

business, export, import, and general licensing issues to the Treasury Department's Office of Foreign Assets Control and the Commerce Department's Bureau of Industry and Security.

3.6. Embassies, DoS. Embassies and consulates play a critical role in the fight against terrorism by serving as direct conduits to the governments of other nations. Embassies facilitate the USG's efforts to disrupt terrorist networks and to apprehend terrorist individuals. The ambassador, his or her deputy, and other members of the country team, including representatives from other agencies, all play instrumental roles in developing and maintaining good working relations with the host country and pursuing U.S. counterterrorism objectives.

3.6.1. Terrorism Finance Coordinating Officer, Embassy, DoS. Facilitates the efforts to disrupt terrorist networks and to apprehend terrorist. Each embassy has identified a Terrorism Finance Coordination Officer to lead the effort of working with the host governments to detect, disrupt, and deter terrorist financing.

3.7. Bureau of International Organization Affairs (IO), DoS. Develops and implements U.S. counterterrorism policy in the United Nations and other international organizations, serving as DoS primary liaison.

3.8. Bureau of Intelligence and Research (INR), DoS. The INR, drawing on all-source intelligence, provides value-added independent analysis of events to DoS policymakers, ensures that intelligence activities support foreign policy and national security purposes, and serves as the focal point in the DoS for ensuring policy review of sensitive counterintelligence and law enforcement activities. INR's primary mission is to harness intelligence to serve U.S. diplomacy. The bureau also analyzes geographical and international boundary issues.

4. Department of Justice (DoJ)

Has the lead responsibility for the prosecution and investigation of terrorism and terrorist financing offenses under Title 18 USC, section 2332b(f). DoJ is the lead agency for law enforcement and criminal matters related to terrorism overseas and domestically. Within the department, multiple bureaus and offices manage various programs and activities to combat terrorism abroad. The DoJ also works with other USG agencies, foreign government law enforcement organizations and agencies, and multinational organizations in carrying out these programs and activities.

4.1. Bureau of Alcohol, Tobacco, Firearms, and Explosives (ATF), DoJ. Participates in investigations of terrorist financing cases involving alcohol, tobacco, firearms, and explosives.

4.2. Drug Enforcement Administration (DEA), DoJ. Participates in investigations of terrorist financing cases involving narcotics and other illicit drugs.

4.3. Asset Forfeiture and Money Laundering Section (AFMLS), DoJ. Assists in the drafting of money laundering, terrorist financing, and asset forfeiture legislation compliant with international standards for international and regional bodies and foreign governments. Provides legal training and technical assistance to foreign prosecutors and judges, in conjunction with Justice's Office of Overseas Prosecutorial Development, Training and Assistance. Sponsors conferences and seminars on transnational financial crimes such as forfeiting the proceeds of corruption, human trafficking, counterfeiting, and terrorism. Participates in U.S. interagency (IA) assessments of countries' capacity to block, seize, and forfeit terrorist and other criminal assets. AFMLS designs and, with its staff and the assistance of the U.S. Attorneys around the nation, delivers both training and technical assistance,

particularly with respect to the threat of money laundering and asset forfeiture issues.

4.4. Criminal Division, Deputy Assistant Attorney General, DoJ. Is responsible for the design, implementation, and support of law enforcement efforts to combat international terrorism, including legislative initiatives and policies. This includes investigating and prosecuting suspected terrorists for acts of terrorism against U.S. interests worldwide. Develops, coordinates, and prosecutes terrorist financing cases; participates in financial analysis and develops relevant financial tools; promotes international efforts; and delivers training to other nations.

4.5. National Security Division (NSD), DoJ. The core mission of NSD is to coordinate DoS efforts to combat terrorism and protect national security. NSD is responsible for assisting the Attorney General and other senior Department and Executive Branch officials in ensuring that the national security-related activities of the U.S. are consistent with relevant law; overseeing terrorism investigations and prosecutions; and handling counterespionage cases and matters.

4.5.1. Counterterrorism Section (CTS), NSD, Deputy Assistant Attorney General, DoJ. Coordinates with headquarter offices of USG agencies including: Treasury Department, DoS, Intelligence agencies, DHS, and the FBI to facilitate prevention of terrorist activity through daily detection and analysis to provide information and support to the field. CTS provides:
a. Investigative and prosecutorial training and technical assistance to foreign investigators, prosecutors, and judges in conjunction with the Office of Overseas Prosecutorial Development, Training, and Assistance and other DoJ components.

b. Designs and, with its staff and the assistance of the U.S. Attorneys around the nation, delivers both training and technical assistance.

c. Investigates and prosecutes terrorist financing matters, including material support cases, through the Terrorist Financing Task Force.

4.5.1.1. Terrorist Financing Unit (TFU), CTS, National Security Division, Deputy Assistant Attorney General, DoJ.
The TFU is made up of white-collar prosecutors drawn from various Main Justice litigating components and U.S. Attorneys' Offices. Coordinates the terrorist financing enforcement efforts within Justice's National Security Division. The task force works with prosecutors around the country as well as with the FBI's Foreign Terrorist Tracking Task Force and Terrorist Financing Operation Section to disrupt groups and individuals representing terrorist threats. TFU works closely with the FBI's Terrorist Financing Operations Section (TFOS), which draws resources from numerous, federal law enforcement agencies and is devoted to the collection and analysis of information concerning terrorist financing.

4.6. Federal Bureau of Investigation (FBI), DoJ.
Leads all terrorist financing investigations and operations and has the primary responsibility for collecting foreign intelligence and counterintelligence information within the U.S. Provides basic and advanced law enforcement training to foreign governments on a bilateral and regional basis and through ILEAs and the FBI Academy in Quantico, Virginia. Developed a two-week terrorist financing course that was delivered and accepted as the USG's model. Participates in U.S. IA assessments of countries' law enforcement and counterterrorism capabilities.

4.6.1. National Security Branch (NSB), FBI, DoJ.
The NSB structure took effect on September 12, 2005, in response to a directive from the President to the Attorney General. The NSB

consists of the FBI's Counterterrorism Division (CTD), the Counterintelligence Division (CD), the Directorate of Intelligence (DI), and the new Weapons of Mass Destruction (WMD) Directorate.

4.6.2. Counterterrorism Division (CTD), NSB, FBI, DoJ. Is the principal investigative agency of the federal government, it serves as lead agency for international counterterrorism investigations. The mission of the CTD is to identify and disrupt potential terrorist plots by individuals or terror cells; to freeze terrorist finances; to share information with law enforcement and intelligence partners worldwide; and to provide strategic and operational threat analysis to the wider intelligence community. The FBI has extraterritorial jurisdiction to expand its investigative authority outside U.S. borders. Its investigations include incidents involving bombings, hostage taking, homicides of U.S. citizens overseas, sabotage, and extortion by threatening the use of WMD.

4.6.2.1. Terrorist Financing Operations Section (TFOS), Counterterrorism Division, NSB, FBI, DoJ. TFOS is both an operational and coordinating entity with proactive and reactive responsibilities. As a coordinating entity, TFOS is responsible for ensuring that a unified approach is pursued in investigating terrorist financing networks by a) coordinating the financial aspects of FBI Field Office and Legal terrorism investigations; b) establishing overall initiatives, policy and guidance on terrorist financing matters; c) participating in the Sub-CSG on Terrorist Financing; d) coordinating national liaison with the financial services sector; e) cooperating in and coordinating criminal terrorist financing investigations with the DoJ; and f) providing support and training to Field Offices, to include the designated Terrorism Financing Coordinator (TFC). According to the FBI, TFOS brings financial expertise to bear in identifying terrorist financing methods and movement of money into and out of the U.S. in support of terrorist activity.

116

To help prevent terrorist attacks, TFOS developed a centralized terrorist financial database to identify potential terrorist-related activity in the U.S. and abroad.

4.6.2.2. National Joint Terrorism Task Force (NJTTF), Counterterrorism Division, NSB, FBI, DoJ. In July 2002, the FBI formally created the NJTTF to act as a liaison and conduit for information on threats and leads from FBI Headquarters to the local JTTFs and to 40 participating agencies. NJTTF serves as the national coordinating mechanism for sharing information on suspected terrorists, including those of foreign origin. Also, it complements the local Joint Terrorism Task Forces by improving collaboration and information sharing with other federal, state, tribal, and local agencies. The task force operates out of the FBI's Strategic Information Operation Center in Washington, D.C.

4.6.3. Foreign Terrorist Tracking Task Force (FTTTF), FBI, DoJ. The FTTTF was established to ensure that federal agencies, including the FBI, INS, Customs Service and others, coordinate their efforts to bar from the U.S. all aliens who meet any of the following criteria: a) aliens who are representatives, members, or supporters of terrorist organizations; b) aliens who are suspected of engaging in terrorist activity; or c) aliens who provide material support to terrorist activity. Federal agencies coordinate programs to accomplish the following: a) deny entry into the U.S. of aliens associated with, suspected of being engaged in, or supporting terrorist activity and b) locate, detain, prosecute, or deport any such aliens already present in the U.S.

4.6.4. Joint Terrorism Task Forces (JTTFs), Field Offices, FBI, DoJ. JTTFs were established in the 1980s and grew significantly after 9/11. The JTTFs serve three main purposes: a) prevent terrorist attacks; b) respond to and investigate terrorist incidents or terrorist-related activity, including terrorist financing; and c) identify and investigate domestic and foreign terrorist groups and individuals targeting or operating within the U.S. JTTFs team up police officers, FBI agents, and officials from over 20 federal law enforcement agencies to investigate terrorism cases. The FBI has increased multi-agency JTTFs from 35 to 101 since 2001 and has increased the number of agents and law enforcement personnel serving on JTTFs from under 1,000 to nearly 4,000. In 2002, the FBI created a national JTTF in Washington, D.C., to collect terrorism information and intelligence and funnel it to the field JTTFs, various terrorism units within the FBI, and partner agencies. Serves as the operational arm of the Antiterrorism Task Forces (ATTFs).

4.7. Anti-Terrorism Advisory Council, U.S. Attorney District Offices, DoJ. Integrates and coordinates the antiterrorism activities in each of the judicial districts within the U.S. The task forces are comprised of federal prosecutors from the U.S. Attorneys Office, members of federal law enforcement agencies, and the primary state and local enforcement officials in each district. They serve as part of a national network that coordinates closely with the JTTF in the collection, analysis, and dissemination of information. The ATTF also developed the U.S. investigative and prosecution strategy throughout the country.

4.8. Office of Overseas Prosecutorial Development, Training and Assistance (OPDAT), DoJ. Provides targeted legal and prosecutorial training and technical assistance for criminal justice sector counterparts abroad and through ILEAs in drafting anti-money-laundering and counteringterrorism-financing statutes. Provides Resident Legal Advisors to focus on developing counterterrorism legislation that criminalizes terrorist financing and achieves other objectives. Conducts regional conferences on terrorist financing, including a focus on charitable organizations. Participates in U.S. interagency assessments to determine countries' criminal justice system capabilities. Since 2002, the Department has provided assistance in countering-terrorism-financing and anti-moneylaundering legislation drafts for 138 countries.

4.9. U.S. National Central Bureau of the International Criminal Police Organization (INTERPOL), DoJ. Represents the U.S. as a member of INTERPOL. It facilitates international law enforcement cooperation by transmitting law enforcement-related information between the National Central Bureaus of INTERPOL, member countries, and U.S. law enforcement agencies. It also coordinates information relevant to international investigations and identifies patterns and trends in criminal activities.

5. Department of Homeland Security (DHS)

The DHS is primarily focused on combating terrorism within the U.S. Within the department, multiple bureaus, offices, and agencies manage various programs and activities to combat terrorism primarily through the Bureau of Immigration and Customs Enforcement and the U.S. Secret Service. However, for selected overseas activities, it supports the DoS. DHS also works with other USG agencies, foreign government organizations and agencies, and international organizations in carrying out counterterrorism programs and activities.

5.1. Bureau of Immigration and Customs Enforcement (ICE), DHS. ICE has a mission to target current terrorist funding sources and identify possible future sources. The bureau has a multi-agency entity called Operation Green Quest to bring together federal agency expertise across departments and bureaus to identify systems, individuals, and organizations that serve as sources of terrorist funding. ICE provides law and border enforcement training and technical assistance to foreign governments in conjunction with other U.S. law enforcement agencies (LEAs) and the ILEAs. ICE also participates in assessments of foreign countries in the law and border enforcement arena. ICE has a long history of collecting, analyzing and utilizing BSA data in criminal investigations. ICE uses Currency Transaction Report (CTR) data as a valuable analytic tool for detecting illegal activity, developing leads, and furthering investigations.

5.1.1. Trade Transparency Unit (TTU), ICE, DHS. The TTU and Money Laundering Coordination Center (MLCC) provide the analytical infrastructure to support financial and trade investigations. The TTU develops investigative leads from analysis through Data Analysis & Research for Trade Transparency System (DARTTS) and facilitates the dissemination of investigative referrals to field entities. The TTU provides the capability to identify and analyze complex trade-based money laundering systems, such as the estimated 5 billion U.S. Dollars (USDs) per year drug money laundering scheme known as the Black Market Peso Exchange.

5.1.2. Financial Operations Unit (Financial Operations) ICE, DHS. Financial Operations provides programmatic support and line authority to ICE Financial field components targeting money-laundering activities. Financial Operations provides ICE's input for the development and utilization of the National Money Laundering Strategy as a foundation to target transnational money laundering activity. Financial Operations also closely coordinates with other law enforcement entities such as FinCEN to assist in processing field requests, including BSA data, USA Patriot Act 314(a) requests for bank account information, and registration data pertaining to money service businesses (MSBs).

5.2. U.S. Secret Service, DHS. The U.S. Secret Service is responsible for enforcement of laws relating to U.S. securities and financial crimes. Its efforts to combat terrorist financing rest primarily on the investigation of counterfeiting of currency and securities.

5.3. **Bureau of Customs and Border Protection, DHS.**
Detects movement of bulk cash across U.S. borders and maintains data about movement of commodities into and out of the U.S.

6. **Department of Defense (DoD)**
The Secretary of Defense is responsible for supporting:
a. The lead federal agency, the DoS, in responding to a terrorist incident overseas
b. The DoJ (through the FBI) for crisis management of a domestic terrorist incident
c. The Federal Emergency Management Agency (FEMA) for consequence management of a domestic terrorist incident.
The DoD has work underway to support efforts in the area of threat finance. While terrorist financing focuses on organizations, cells, and individuals directly linked to terrorism, threat financing is a broader-based concept and includes WMD funding, terrorist financing, narcotics-trafficking, organized crime, and human trafficking. The DoD has stated that following the money (in all forms) is a key element to mapping the network and understanding relationships between nodes and a key enabler for achieving DoD objectives. The DoD views the Treasury Department as the lead agency for terrorist finances.

6.1. **U.S. Special Operations Command (USSOCOM), DoD.**
USSOCOM has been designated the executive agent for the DoD Global War on Terrorism Campaign. USSOCOM synchronizes the counterterrorism plans of the five geographic military commands as components of a global campaign.

6.1.1. **USSOCOM Threat Finance Exploitation Branch, USSOCOM, DoD.** Was established to coordinate and integrate military operations with IA activities to reduce threats to the U.S. and U.S. interests abroad by synchronizing joint DoD, IA, and coalition intelligence collection and analysis activities that

lead to detection, identification, targeting, disruption, or destruction of terrorist financial support systems and networks. They serve as the DoD focal point for terrorist exploitation among the USG.

6.2. Geographic Combatant Commands (GCC) – Threat Financing Exploitation Units (TFEUs), GCC, DoD. Currently, USCENTCOM, USEUCOM, USNORTHCOM, USPACOM, and USSOUTHCOM are the operating TFEUs which work with DoD and non-DoD intelligence, law enforcement and regulatory agencies to: a) detect financial support networks; b) collect, process and analyze information; and c) target, disrupt, or destroy financial systems and networks which support activities that threaten U.S. interests. Not all the GCCs call their TF Exploitation entity a TFEU. For instance USSOCOM calls its entity a TF Exploitation Branch, but each GCC has an entity that analyzes and exploits financial intelligence. Each of the TF Exploitation entities has a somewhat different focus that is based on their region. For example, USSOUTHCOM is more focused on the narcotics trafficking portion of TF, whereas USCENTCOM is focused more on the terrorists and insurgents. Each of the TF Exploitation entities are resourced, manned, and utilized to varying degrees based on the emphasis that is placed on their importance by the GCC, and not all TF Exploitation entities operate at the same level of proficiency.

6.3. Defense Intelligence Agency (DIA), DoD. DIA is a DoD combat support agency and an important member of the United States Intelligence Community. DIA is a major producer and manager of foreign military intelligence and provides military intelligence to war fighters, defense policymakers and force planners, in the DoD and the Intelligence Community, in support of U.S. military planning and operations and weapon systems acquisition.

6.3.1. **Joint Intelligence Task Force-Combating Terrorism (JITF-CT), DIA, DoD.** Provides enhanced analysis and production to support worldwide efforts in counterterrorism. JITF-CT analysts produced daily assessments of possible terrorist threats to DoD personnel, facilities, and interests. In addition, the Defense Intelligence Analysis Program (DIAP) mandated the responsibility of threat finance analysis be given to JITF-CT.

7. **Office of the Director of National Intelligence Agency (ODNI).** The ODNI was established through the Intelligence Reform and Terrorism Prevention Act of 2004. The Director of National Intelligence (DNI), who must be confirmed by the U.S. Senate, does not serve as the head of any individual element within the U.S. intelligence community, but establishes objectives and priorities for the intelligence community and manages and directs tasking of collection, analysis, production, and dissemination of national intelligence.

7.1. **Central Intelligence Agency (CIA), ODNI.** The Director of the CIA serves as the head of the CIA and reports to the DNI. To accomplish its mission, the CIA engages in research, development, and deployment of high-leverage technology for intelligence purposes. As a separate agency, the CIA serves as an independent source of analysis on topics of concern and works closely with the other organizations in the IC to ensure that the intelligence consumer, whether Washington policy maker or battlefield commander, receives the best intelligence possible.

8. **Interagency.** Interagency organizations are listed, followed by their participants and description of their effort.
8.1. **National Counterterrorism Center (NCTC), ODNI.** *CIA, DoJ, FBI, DoD, DHS, DoS, Treasury Department, Department of Agriculture, Department of Energy, Department of Health and Human Services, National Geospatial-*

Intelligence Agency, Nuclear Regulatory Commission and U.S. Capitol Police.

The NCTC, formally The Terrorist Threat Integration Center (TTIC), is staffed by personnel from across the USG and serves as the primary organization in the USG for integrating and analyzing all intelligence pertaining to terrorism and counterterrorism and conducting strategic operational planning by integrating all instruments of national power. In December 2004, Congress codified the NCTC in the Intelligence Reform and Terrorism Prevention Act (IRTPA) and placed the NCTC in the Office of the ODNI. The NCTC is a multi-agency organization dedicated to eliminating the terrorist threat to U.S. interests at home and abroad. NCTC is charged with ensuring that agencies, as appropriate, have access to and receive all-source intelligence necessary to execute their counterterrorism plans and perform independent, alternative analysis. The NCTC was designed to serve as a central knowledge bank for information about known and suspected terrorists and to coordinate and monitor counterterrorism plans and activities of all the government agencies. The NCTC is also responsible for preparing the daily terrorism threat report for the President.

8.2. Terrorist Finance Working Group (TFWG). *DoS, Treasury Department, DoJ, DHS. Other participants include NSC, CIA, Federal Deposit Insurance Corporation and the Federal Reserve.*

TFWG is co-chaired by S/CT and INL. It meets biweekly to receive intelligence briefings, schedule assessment trips, review assessment reports, and discuss the development and implementation of technical assistance and training programs. TFWG leads the Program Development Process, which, with input from the intelligence and law enforcement communities, DoS, Treasury, and DoJ:

a. Identifies and prioritize countries needing the most assistance to deal with terrorist financing.

b. Evaluates priority countries' counterterrorism finance and anti-money-laundering regimes.

c. Prepares a formal assessment report on vulnerabilities to terrorist financing and makes recommendations for training and technical assistance to address these weaknesses.

d. Develops a counterterrorism financing training implementation plan based on FSAT recommendations.

e. Provides sequenced training and technical assistance to priority countries in-country, regionally, or in the U.S.

f. Encourages burden sharing with U.S. allies; with international financial institutions, such as the International Monetary Fund (IMF), World Bank, and regional development banks; and through international organizations such as the United Nations, the United Nations Counterterrorism Committee, FATF on Money Laundering, and the Group of Eight (G-8) to capitalize on and maximize international efforts to strengthen counterterrorism finance efforts.

8.2.2. Financial Systems Assessment Team (FSAT). *DoS, DoJ, and Treasury Department.*

DoS has the lead for FSAT teams. FSAT teams of 6–8 members include technical experts from State, Treasury, Justice, and other regulatory and law enforcement agencies and evaluate priority countries' counterterrorism finance and anti-money-laundering regimes. The FSAT onsite visits take about one week and include in-depth meetings with host government financial regulatory agencies, the judiciary, law enforcement agencies, the private financial services sector, and nongovernmental organizations.

8.3. Terrorism Financial Review Group (TFRG). *CIA, DoJ, FBI, DoD, DHS, DoS, Treasury Department.*

The mission of the TFRG has evolved into a broad effort to identify, investigate, prosecute, disrupt, and dismantle all terrorist-related financial and fundraising activities. The TFRG has taken a leadership role in coordinating the comprehensive financial investigative effort. To accomplish this mission, it has implemented initiatives to address all aspects of terrorist financing. The TFRG:

a. Conducts full financial analyses of terrorist suspects and their global financial support structures.

b. Coordinates liaison and outreach efforts to exploit financial resources of private, government and foreign entities.

c. Uses FBI and Legal expertise and relationships to develop financial information from foreign law enforcement and private agencies.

d. Works jointly with the law enforcement, regulatory, and ICs.

e. Develops predictive models and mines data to proactively identify terrorist suspects.

f. Provides the financial component to classified counterterrorism investigations in support of the FBI's counterterrorism responsibilities.

8.4. **Multiple, International Law Enforcement Academies.**
DoS, DoJ, DHS, and Treasury Department.

International Law Enforcement Academies are regional academies led by U.S. agencies partnering with foreign governments to provide law enforcement training, including anti-money-laundering and counteringterrorism-financing. International Law Enforcement Academies in Gaborone, Botswana; Bangkok, Thailand; Budapest, Hungary; and Roswell, New Mexico, train over 2,300 participants annually on topics such as criminal investigations, international banking and money laundering, drug-trafficking, human smuggling, and cyber-crime.

APPENDIX D: International Organizations and Efforts to Disrupt Terrorist Financing

(Adapted from the "Terrorist Financing: Better Strategic Planning Needed to Coordinate U.S. Efforts to Deliver Counterterrorism Financing Training and Technical Assistance Abroad: GAO-06-19," 2005, GAO Reports 1, 39-43.)

1. International Standard Setters

1.1. United Nations (UN). Of the key international entities, the UN has the broadest range of membership and the ability to adopt treaties or international conventions that have the effect of law in a country once signed and ratified, depending on a country's constitution (which is the case in the U.S.).

1.1.1. Counterterrorism Implementation Task Force (CTITF). The CTITF's overall function is to coordinate the various UN bodies working on counterterrorism. CTITF was created by the Secretary General and encompasses the UN Secretariat and the wider UN system in an attempt to better coordinate counterterrorism efforts across the UN system and to ensure stronger cooperation and efficiency in implementing the counterterrorism-related mandates of various UN departments, programs, funds, offices and agencies and to strengthen information sharing throughout the system. In its coordinating work the Task Force goes beyond the wider UN system to also include 24 other entities, such as the International Criminal Police Organization (INTERPOL) and IMF.

1.1.2. Counterterrorism Committee (CTC). Was established via Security Council Resolution 1373 to monitor the performance of the member countries in building a global capacity against terrorism. The CTC, which is comprised of the 15 members of the Security Council, is not a law enforcement agency; it does not issue sanctions, nor does it prosecute or condemn individual countries. Rather, the committee seeks to establish a dialogue between the Security Council and member countries on how to achieve the objectives of Resolution 1373. Countries submit a report to the CTC on steps taken to implement resolution's measures and report regularly on progress. CTC identifies weaknesses and facilitates assistance, but does not provide direct assistance. The CTC's primary task is the review of member state reports that describe the degree of national compliance with the counterterrorism mandates of Security Council Resolution 1373. As of 18 January 2002, 122 nation-states had submitted reports to the committee.

1.1.2.1. **Counterterrorism Committee Executive Directorate (CTED).** Provides the CTC with expert advice on all areas covered by resolution 1373. CTED was established also with the aim of facilitating technical assistance to countries, as well as promoting closer cooperation and coordination both within the UN system of organizations and among regional and intergovernmental bodies.

1.1.3. **The UN Global Counterterrorism Strategy (2006).** Enhances national, regional, and international efforts in counterterrorism. This is the first time that all 192 member states have agreed to a common strategic approach to fight terrorism. Several items of the Strategy address terrorist financing:
a. Under measures to prevent and combat terrorism, item 1 addresses refraining from financing, encouraging or tolerating terrorist activities; item 2 addresses cooperating fully in the fight against persons who support, facilitate, participate or attempt to participate in the financing, of terrorist acts; and item 10 encourages states to implement the standards embodied in the FATF Forty Recommendations on Money Laundering and Nine Special Recommendations on Terrorist Financing.

b. Under measures to build states' capacity to prevent and combat terrorism, item 8 encourages the IMF, World Bank, the UN Office on Drugs and Crime (UNODC) and INTERPOL to enhance cooperation to help states comply with international norms and obligations to combat terrorist financing.

c. Rule of law, item 4, addresses maintaining effective rule so that any persons who supports terrorist acts is brought to justice.

1.1.4. Global Program Against Money Laundering (GPML) (1997). The GPML is within the UNODC. The GPML is a research and assistance project with the goal of increasing the effectiveness of international action against money laundering by offering technical expertise, training, and advice to member countries upon request. It focuses its efforts in the following areas:

a. Raising the awareness level among key persons in UN member states

b. Helping create legal frameworks with the support of model legislation

c. Developing institutional capacity, in particular with the creation of financial intelligence units

d. Providing training for legal, judicial, law enforcement, regulators,and private financial sectors including computer-based training

e. Promoting a regional approach to addressing problems

f. Maintaining strategic relationships

g. Maintaining database and performing analysis of relevant information.

1.2 Financial Action Task Force on Money Laundering (FATF). The FATF was formed in 1989 by the G-7 countries. FATF is an intergovernmental body comprised of 33 member jurisdictions and two regional organizations that brings together legal, financial, and law enforcement experts and whose purpose is to develop, promote, and asses policies, both at the national and international levels, to combat money laundering and the financing of terrorism (expanded to include counterterrorism financing in October 2001). FATF has developed multiple partnerships with international and regional organizations in order to constitute a global network of organizations against money laundering and terrorist financing. Five of the FATF's most notable contributions to disrupt terrorist financing include:

a. Forty Recommendations on Money Laundering

b. Nine Special Recommendations on Terrorist Financing

c. The establishment of the Non-Cooperative Countries and Territories (NCCT) List

d. Monitoring member progress in implementing anti-money-laundering measures

e. Reporting on money laundering trends and techniques.

1.2.1. **Forty Recommendations on Money Laundering.** The FATF's Forty Recommendations constitute a comprehensive framework for anti-money laundering (AML) and are designed for universal application by countries throughout the world. The Forty Recommendations set out principles for action, which permit a country's flexibility in implementing the principles according to the country's own particular circumstances and constitutional requirements. Although not binding as law upon a country, the Forty Recommendations have been widely endorsed by the international community and relevant organizations as the international standard for AML. The Forty Recommendations are actually mandates for action by a country if that country wants to be viewed by the international community as meeting international standards. The Forty Recommendations are available at www. fatf-gafi.org.

1.2.2. **Nine Special Recommendations on Terrorist Financing.** The FATF's Nine Special Recommendations, which have become the international standard for evaluating a state's antiterrorist financing laws, require:

a. Ratifying the *United Nations International Convention for the Suppression of the Financing of Terrorism* and implementing relevant UN resolutions against terrorist financing

b.. Criminalizing the financing of terrorism, terrorist acts, and terrorist organizations

c. Freezing and confiscating terrorist assets

d. Reporting by financial institutions of suspicious transactions linked to terrorism

e. Providing the widest possible assistance to other countries' laws enforcement and regulatory authorities for terrorist financing investigations

f. Imposing anti-money-laundering requirements on alternative remittance systems

g. Including accurate and meaningful originator information on money transfers by financial institutions

h. Ensuring that nonprofit organizations cannot be misused to finance terrorism

i. Implementing measures to detect the physical cross-border transportation of currency and bearer negotiable instruments.

1.2.3. **The Non-Cooperative Countries and Territories (NCCT) List.** One of FATF's objectives is to promote the adoption of international antimoney-laundering/countering-terrorism-financing standards by all countries. Thus, its mission extends beyond its own membership. However, FATF can only sanction its member countries and territories. Thus, in order to encourage all countries to adopt measures to prevent, detect, and prosecute money launderers (i.e., to implement the Forty Recommendations), FATF adopted a process to identify noncooperative countries and territories that serve as obstacles to international cooperation in this area and place them on a public list. An NCCT country is encouraged to make rapid progress in remedying its deficiencies or countermeasures may be imposed which may include specific actions by FATF member countries. Most countries make a concerted effort to be taken off the NCCT list because it causes significant problems to their international business and reputation.

1.2.4. **Monitoring Member's Progress.** Facilitated by a two-stage process: self assessments and mutual evaluations. In the self-assessment stage, each member annually responds to a standard questionnaire regarding its implementation of the recommendations. In the mutual evaluation stage, each member is examined and assessed by experts from other member countries. Ultimately, if a member country does not take steps to achieve compliance, membership in the organization can be suspended. There is, however, a sense of peer pressure and a process of graduated steps before these sanctions are enforced.

1.2.5. **Reporting on Money Laundering Trends and Techniques.** One of FATF's functions is to review and report on money laundering trends, techniques, and methods (also referred to as typologies). To accomplish this aspect of its mission, FATF issues annual reports on developments in money laundering through its Typologies Report. These reports are very useful for all countries, not just FATF members, to keep current with new techniques or trends to launder money and for other developments in this area.

2. International Capacity Builders

2.1 **Egmont Group of Financial Intelligence Units.** This is an is an informal body without a secretariat. The Egmont Group is an international network of 101 countries that have implemented national centers to collect information on suspicious or unusual financial activity from the financial industry, analyze the data, and make it available to appropriate authorities and other FIUs for use in combating terrorist financing and other financial crimes. Members of the Egmont Group have access to a secure private Web site to exchange information. As of 2004, 87 of the members were connected to the secure Web. The Egmont Group has no permanent location and meets in a plenary session once a year and in working group sessions three times a year. Within the Egmont Group, the FIU heads make all the policy decisions, including membership. Currently, Egmont Group's efforts focus on fostering improved communications, information sharing, and training coordination worldwide in the fight against money laundering and terrorist financing.

2.1.1 **Financial Intelligence Unites (FIUs).** FIUs are a central, national agencies responsible for receiving (and as permitted, requesting), analyzing, and disseminating to competent authorities, disclosures of financial information concerning suspected proceeds of crime and potential financing of terrorism or as required by national legislation or regulation in order to combat money laundering and terrorist financing. The Egmont Group's definition of an FIU is entirely consistent with the Forty Recommendations of the FATF. In addition, FIUs must also commit to act in accordance with the Egmont Group's Principles for Information Exchange Between FIUs for money laundering and terrorist financing cases. These principles include conditions for the exchange of information, limitation on permitted uses of information, and confidentiality.

2.2 **International Monetary Fund (IMF) and World Bank.** The World Bank helps countries strengthen development efforts by providing loans and technical assistance for institutional capacity building. The IMF mission involves financial surveillance and the promotion of international monetary stability. Together, the World Bank and IMF have established a collaborative framework with the FATF for conducting comprehensive anti-money-laundering/combating-financing-ofterrorism (AML/CFT) assessments of countries' compliance with the FATF's Forty Recommendations on Money Laundering and Nine Special Recommendations on

Terrorist Financing (known as the FATF 40 + 9 Recommendations) using a single global methodology. The assessments are carried out as part of the Financial Sector Assessment Program (FSAP) and lead to a Report on Observance of Standard and Codes (ROSCs). Three areas that the World Bank and IMF focus on include research and analysis and awareness-raising, assessments, and training and technical assistance.

2.2.1. **Research and Analysis and Awareness-Raising.** The World Bank and IMF have: a) conducted work on international practices in implementing anti-money-laundering and countering-terrorism-financing regimes; b) issued Analysis of the Hawala System discussing implications for regulatory and supervisory response; c) developed a comprehensive reference guide on anti-money-laundering/countering-terrorismfinancing presenting all relevant information in one source; d) conducted Regional Policy Global Dialogue series with country, World Bank and IMF, development banks, and FATF-style regional bodies covering challenges, lessons learned, and assistance needed; and e) developed Country Assistance Strategies that cover anti-money laundering and countering-terrorism financing in greater detail in countries that have been deficient in meeting international standards.

2.2.2. **Assessments.** The World Bank and IMF have a) worked in close collaboration with FATF and FATF-style regional bodies to a produce single comprehensive methodology for anti-money-laundering/ countering-terrorism-financing assessments and b) engaged in a successful pilot program of assessments of country compliance with FATF recommendations. In 2004, the World Bank and IMF adopted the FATF 40 + 9 Recommendations as one of the 12 standards and codes for which Reports on the Observance of Standards and Codes can be prepared and made anti-money-laundering/countering-terrorism-financing assessments a regular part of IMF/World Bank work. World Bank and IMF staff participated in 58 of the 92 assessments conducted since 2002.In addition, the Boards of the World Bank and the IMF have agreed to adopt a more comprehensive and integrated approach to conducting assessments of compliance with international standards for fighting money laundering and terrorist financing in member countries and to step up the delivery of technical assistance to those countries whose financial systems are most at risk.

2.2.3. **Training and Technical Assistance.** The World Bank and IMF have: a) organized training conferences and workshops, b) delivered technical assistance to individual countries, c) coordinated technical assistance, and d) substantially increased technical assistance to member countries on strengthening legal, regulatory, and financial supervisory frameworks for anti-money-laundering/counteringterrorism-financing. In 2002-2003 there were 85 country-specific technical projects benefiting 63 countries and 32 projects reaching more than 130 countries. Between January 2004 and June 2005, the World Bank and IMF delivered an additional 210 projects. In 2004, IMF and the World Bank decided to expand the anti-money-laundering/countering-terrorism-financing technical assistance work to cover the full scope of the expanded FATF recommendations following the successful pilot program of assessments.

2.3 **International Organization of Supreme Audit Institutions.** International cooperation related to money laundering also occurs through the International Organization of Supreme Audit Institutions, which represents 191 UN member nations and is the top accountability organization related to government audit and oversight. The U.S. Government Accountability Office (formerly *General Accounting Office*) and its counterparts from around the world are working cooperatively to improve their oversight capacity for government departments and regulatory financial institutions. This work takes the form of publishing and disseminating standards and guidelines in critical areas such as auditing, internal control, financial reporting, information technology, and public debt. In addition, the organization recently established a task force charged with studying the national audit offices' role in helping prevent and detect money laundering and sharing information and experiences with each other. The organization also has established partnerships with organizations such as the World Bank and the International Federation of Accountants to strengthen its impact in these areas.

2.4 **G8.** The G8 established a Counterterrorism Action Group (CTAG) composed of donor countries, as well as other states, mainly donors, to expand and coordinate training and assistance for countries that have the political will but lack the capacity to combat terror.

CTAG provides an active forum for donor countries to coordinate counterterrorism cooperation with and assistance for countries in support of the UN Counterterrorism Committee's efforts to oversee implementation of UN Security Council Resolution 1373. This resolution obligates all states to deny safe haven to those who finance, plan, support, or commit terrorist acts. CTAG has coordinated efforts to assist countries to assess and improve airport security and has promoted and assisted with the implementation of travel security and facilitation standards and practices developed by G8's Secure and Facilitated International Travel Initiative (SAFTI). CTAG goals are to analyze and prioritize needs and expand training and assistance in critical areas, including counterterrorism financing and other counterterrorism areas. In 2004, CTAG coordinated with FATF to obtain assessments of countries CTAG identified as priorities. Anticipated areas of activity include outreach to countries in the area of counterterrorism cooperation and providing capacity building assistance to nations with insufficient capacity to fight terrorism.

2.5. **INTERPOL.** INTERPOL's Web site serves as a clearinghouse for foreign law enforcement for the lists of those subject to freezing actions. The INTERPOL database consolidates international and national lists of terrorist financiers and makes it available to police around the world to prevent the flow of funds to terrorist groups and to assist in criminal investigations. INTERPOL collects, stores, analyzes, and exchanges information about suspected individuals and groups and their activities. The organization, with its 186 member states, also coordinates the circulation of alerts and warnings on terrorists, dangerous criminals, and weapons threats to police in member countries. A chief initiative in this area is the Fusion Task Force.

2.5.1. **Fusion Task Force (FTF).** As the planning for terrorist attacks often spans multiple countries and regions, fighting terrorism also requires the same level of effort and cooperation among nations. Spearheading INTERPOL's antiterrorism efforts is the FTF, created in September 2002, in the wake of the alarming rise in the scale and sophistication of international terrorist attacks. FTF's primary objectives are to:
a. Identify active terrorist groups and their membership.
b. Solicit, collect, and share information and intelligence.
c. Provide analytical support.
d. Enhance the capacity of member countries to address the threats of terrorism and organized crime.

As terrorist organizations' far-reaching activities are inextricably linked, the task force investigates not only attacks but also organizational hierarchies, training, financing, methods, and motives.

3. **Regional Entities**

In addition to the International Standard Setters and Capacity Builders there are other international organizations that play crucial roles in the fight against money laundering and terrorist financing. These groups tend to be organized according to geographic region or by the special purpose of the organization.

3.1. FATF-Style Regional Bodies (FSRBs). Modeled after FATF, these groups have anti-money-laundering/countering-terrorism-financing efforts as their objectives. FSRBs encourage implementation and enforcement of FATF's 40 + 9 Recommendations. They administer mutual evaluations of their members, which are intended to identify weaknesses so that the members may take remedial action. They provide members information about trends, techniques, and other developments for money laundering in their typology reports. The size, sophistication, and the degree to which the FSRBs can carry out their missions vary greatly. Currently, the eight FSRBs are Asia/Pacific Group on Money Laundering, Caribbean Financial Action Task Force, Council of Europe MONEYVAL, Eastern and Southern African Anti-Money Laundering Group, Eurasian Group on Combating Money Laundering and Financing of Terrorism, Financial Action Task Force Against Money Laundering in South America, Middle East and North Africa Financial Action Task Force, Inter-governmental Action Group Against Money Laundering (West Africa).

3.2. Wolfsberg Group of Banks. The Wolfsberg Group is an association of 12 global banks, representing primarily international private banking concerns. The group was named after the Château Wolfsberg in northeastern Switzerland where the group was formed. Wolfsberg Group established four sets of principles for private banking:
a. AML principles for private banking, which deal with customer identification, including establishing beneficial

ownership for all accounts, and situations involving extra due diligence, such as unusual or suspicious transactions

b. A statement on the suppression of the financing of terrorism, which emphasizes that financial institutions need to assist competent authorities in fighting terrorist financing through prevention, detection, and information sharing

c. Fourteen AML principles for correspondent banking, which prohibit international banks from doing business with "shell banks" and use a risk-based approach to correspondent banking that is designed to ascertain the appropriate level of due diligence that a bank should adopt with regard to its correspondent banking clients

d. Monitoring screening and searching, which identifies issues that should be addressed in order for financial institutions to develop suitable monitoring, screening and searching processes, using a risk-based profile approach.

3.3. The Commonwealth Secretariat. The Commonwealth Secretariat is a voluntary association of 53 sovereign states that consult and cooperate in the common interest of their peoples on a broad range of topics, including the promotion of international understanding and world peace. All of the member states, except for Mozambique, have experienced direct or indirect British rule or have been linked administratively to another Commonwealth country.

With regard to AML and combating the financing of terrorism, the Commonwealth Secretariat provides assistance to countries to implement the FATF 40 + 9 Recommendations. It works with national and international organizations and assists governments in the implementation of the FATF recommendations. In addition, the Commonwealth Secretariat has published *A Manual of Best Practices for Combating Money Laundering in the Financial Sector*. The manual is for government policy makers, regulators and financial institutions.

3.4. **Organization of American States (OAS).** The OAS is the regional body for security and diplomacy in the Western Hemisphere. All 35 countries of the Americas have ratified the OAS charter. In 2004, the commission amended model regulations for the hemisphere to include techniques to combat terrorist financing, development of a variety of associated training initiatives, and a number of anti-money-laundering/counterterrorism meetings. Its Mutual Evaluation Mechanism included updating and revising some 80 questionnaire indicators through which the countries mutually evaluate regional efforts and projects. Worked with International Development Bank and France to provide training for prosecutors and judges. Based on agreement with Inter-American Development Bank for nearly $2 million, conducted a two-year project to strengthen FIUs in eight countries. In addition, the OAS assists with evaluating strategic plans and advising on technical design for FIUs in region.

3.5. **Asian Development Bank (ADB).** Established in 1966, the ADB is a multilateral development finance institution dedicated to reducing poverty in Asia and the Pacific. The bank is owned by 63 members, mostly from the region, and engages in mostly public sector lending in its developing member countries.

According to the ADB, it was one of the first multilateral development banks to address the money laundering problem, directly and indirectly, through regional and country assistance programs. The ADB Policy Paper, adopted on 1 April 2003, has three key elements: a) assisting developing member countries in establishing and implementing effective legal and institutional systems for anti-money-laundering and countering-terrorism-financing, b) increasing collaboration with other international organizations and aid agencies, and c) strengthening internal controls to safeguard ADB's funds. The bank provides loans and technical assistance for a broad range of development activities, including strengthening and developing anti-money-laundering regimes.

3.6. European Union (EU). The EU and the U.S. have worked closely together to ensure that terrorist financiers designated by one party are also designated by the other. For example, in August 2002, Italy joined the U.S. in submitting to the UN Sanctions Committee the names of 25 individuals and entities linked to Al Qaeda so that their assets could be frozen worldwide.

4. Industry Sector Standard Setters
The following are various industries that are viewed as international standard setters.

4.1. Basel Committee on Banking (Basel Committee). Established by the central bank Governors of the Group of Ten countries in 1974, formulates broad supervisory standards and guidelines and recommends statements of best practice in the expectation that individual authorities will take steps to implement them through detailed arrangements— statutory or otherwise—which are best suited to their own national systems. Three of the Basel Committee's supervisory standards and guidelines concern money laundering issues:

a. *Statement on Prevention of Criminal Use of the Banking System for the purpose of Money Laundering*, 1988, which outlines basic policies and procedures that bank managers should ensure are in place

b. *Core Principles for Effective Banking Supervision*, 1997, which provides a comprehensive blueprint for an effective bank supervisory system and covers a wide range of topics including money laundering

c. *Customer Due Diligence*, 2001, which also strongly supports adoption and implementation of the FATF recommendations.

4.2. International Association of Insurance Supervisors.
Established in 1994, this is an organization of supervisors from
more than 100 different countries and jurisdictions that
promotes cooperation among regulators, sets international
standards, provides training, and coordinates with other
financial sectors.

The Association established the *Anti-Money Laundering
Guidance Notes for Insurance Supervisors and Insurance
Entities*, 2002, which is a comprehensive discussion on money
laundering in the context of the insurance industry. The
guidance is intended to be implemented by individual countries
taking into account the particular insurance companies
involved, the products offered within the country, and the
country's own financial system. The Association's work is
consistent with the FATF 40 + 9 Recommendations and the
Basel Core Principles for Effective Banking Supervision. Its
2002 paper was updated as a *Guidance Paper on Anti-Money
Laundering and Combating the Financing of Terrorism* in
2004, with cases on money laundering and terrorist financing.
A document based upon these cases is posted on their Website
and is updated as new cases that might result from the FATF
typology project are added.

**4.3. International Organization of Securities Commissions
(IOSCO).** Members regulate and administer securities and laws
in their respective 105 national securities commissions. Core
objectives are to protect investors; ensure that markets are fair,
efficient, and transparent; and reduce systematic risk.

IOSCO passed *Resolution on Money Laundering* in 1992
and *Principles on Client Identification and Beneficial
Ownership for the Securities Industry*, 2004, which is a
comprehensive framework relating to customer due-diligence
requirements and complementing the FATF Forty
Recommendations. In addition, IOSCO and FATF have
discussed further steps to strengthen cooperation among FIUs

and securities regulators in order to combat money laundering and terrorist financing.

APPENDIX E. International Resolutions and Conventions

(Data compiled by the author from the UN Web site available at www. un.org (accessed 18 September 2006); INTERPOL Web site available at www.interpol.int/ (accessed 18 September 2006), and based on government, industry, and various other research sources.)

1. **United Nations (UN)**

The UN and its member states established a broad array of resolutions and conventions to create a multilateral framework for combating international terrorism. This UN-based multilateral framework falls into three broad categories of documents or agreements:

a. UN conventions or protocols related to terrorism

b. UN Security Council resolutions

c. UN General Assembly resolutions.

According to the DoS, the U.S. is a party to all 12 international conventions and protocols relating to terrorism.

1.1. UN Conventions. International conventions, which require signing, ratification, and implementation by the UN member country to have the effect of law within that country.

1.1.1. International Convention for the Suppression of the Financing of Terrorism, 1999. This convention applies to the offense of direct involvement or complicity in the intentional and unlawful provision or collection of funds, whether attempted or actual, with the intention or knowledge that any part of the funds may be used to carry out any of the offenses described in the conventions listed in its annex, or an act intended to cause death or serious bodily injury to any person not actively involved in armed conflict in order to intimidate a population, or to compel a government or an international organization to do or abstain from doing any act. The provision

144

or collection of funds in this manner is an offense whether or not the funds are actually used to carry out the proscribed acts. The convention requires each state party to take appropriate measures, in accordance with its domestic legal principles, for the detection and freezing, seizure, or forfeiture of any funds used or allocated for the purposes of committing the offences described.

1.1.2. **International Convention Against Transnational Organized Crime (TOC), 2000.** The TOC entered into force on 29 September 2003, after 40 countries became party to the treaty. As of 26 October 2005, there are 147 signatories and 112 parties to the TOC. The trafficking in persons protocol entered into force on 25 December 2003 and has 117 Signatories and 93 Parties. The migrant smuggling protocol entered into force on 28 January 2004 and currently has 112 Signatories and 82 Parties. The TOC represents the first legally binding multilateral instrument that specifically targets transnational organized crime. It requires parties that have not already done so to adopt legislation criminalizing certain conduct typically associated with organized crime and provides a framework for international cooperation among parties to assist each other in investigating and prosecuting transnational organized crime. The successful negotiation and widespread ratification of the TOC represent the global community's resolve to combat transnational organized crime as a serious worldwide threat.

1.1.3. **Convention Against Corruption, 2003.** This is the first legally binding multilateral treaty to address on a global basis the problems relating to corruption. Requires parties to institute a comprehensive domestic regulatory and supervisory regime for banks and financial institutions to deter and detect money laundering. Regimes must emphasize requirements for customer identification, record keeping, and suspicious transaction reporting.

1.2. Security Council Resolutions. Unlike an international convention, which requires signing, ratification, and implementation by the UN member country to have the effect of law within that country, a Security Council Resolution passed in response to a threat to international peace and security under Chapter VII of the UN Charter is binding upon all UN member countries.

1.2.1. Security Council Resolution 1214, 1998. Demands that the Taliban stop providing sanctuary and training for international terrorists and their operations, and that all Afghan factions cooperate with efforts to bring indicted terrorists to justice.

1.2.2. Security Council Resolution 1267, 1999. Obligates member states to freeze assets of individuals and entities associated with Osama bin Laden or members of Al Qaeda or the Taliban that are included on the consolidated list maintained and regularly updated by the UN 1267 Sanctions Committee.

1.2.3. Security Council Resolution 1269, 1999. Calls on member states to implement the international antiterrorist conventions to which they are a party and encourages the speedy adoption of the pending conventions. Although the Security Council specifically referred to "terrorist financing" for the first time in Resolution 1269, it was not in the context of state-sponsored terrorism. General Assembly Resolution 49/60 clearly implicates state entities directly in such financing by acts and omissions such as sheltering, facilitating, funding, and failure to adopt suppressive measures.

1.2.4. Security Council Resolution 1333, 2000. Requires member states to freeze without delay the funds and other financial assets of Osama bin Laden and Al Qaeda associates. It also demands that the Taliban should act swiftly to close all camps where terrorists are trained within the territory under its control.

1.2.5. Security Council Resolution 1363, 2001. Establishes a mechanism to monitor the implementation of the measures imposed by UN Security Council Resolutions 1267 and 1333.

1.2.6. Security Council Resolution 1368, 2001. Condemns the 9/11 attacks and calls on all states to work together urgently to bring to justice the perpetrators, organizers and sponsors of these terrorist attacks and stresses that those responsible for aiding, supporting or harboring the perpetrators, organizers and sponsors of these will be held accountable. The resolution also calls on the international community to increase their efforts to prevent and suppress terrorist acts by increased cooperation and full implementation of the relevant international antiterrorist conventions and Security Council resolutions, especially Resolution 1269 (1999). Finally, the resolution expresses the Security Council's preparedness to take all necessary steps to respond to the terrorist attacks of 9/11 and to combat all forms of terrorism, in accordance with its responsibilities under the charter of the UN.

1.2.7. Security Council Resolution 1373, 2001. Was adopted in direct response to events of September 11, 2001. Obligates countries to criminalize actions to finance terrorism and deny all forms of support, freeze funds or assets of persons, organizations, or entities involved in terrorist acts; prohibit active or passive assistance to terrorists; and cooperate with other countries in criminal investigations and sharing information about planned terrorist acts.

1.2.8. Security Council Resolution 1377, 2001. Calls on member states to implement UN Security Council Resolution 1373 and to assist each other in doing so. Also it invites states to inform the Counterterrorism Committee of areas where they require support.

1.2.9. **Security Council Resolution 1390, 2002.** Obligates member states to freeze assets of individuals and entities associated with Osama bin Laden or members of Al Qaeda or the Taliban that are included on the consolidated list maintained and regularly updated by the UN 1267 Sanctions Committee.

1.2.10. **Security Council Resolution 1452, 2002.** Decided that the provisions of resolution 1267 and 1390 do not apply to funds and other financial assets or economic resources that have been determined by the state to be necessary for basic expenses and extraordinary expenses.

1.2.11. **Security Council Resolution 1455, 2003.** Improves the implementation of measures against the Taliban and members of the Al Qaeda organization and their associates to include: a) the freezing of funds and other financial resources of the Taliban, as well as funds and other financial assets of Osama bin Laden and individuals and entities associated with him as designated by the committee established by resolution 1267 (1999), an arms embargo, and travel prohibitions and b) the need for improved coordination and increased exchange of information between the committee established by resolution 1267 (1999) and the Counterterrorism Committee established by resolution 1373 (2001), and called on all states to submit an updated report to the committee no later than 90 days after today on all steps taken to implement the above-mentioned measures and all related investigations and enforcement actions, unless to do so would compromise investigations or enforcement actions.

1.2.12. **Security Council Resolution 1456, 2003.** Calls on states to prevent and suppress all active and passive support to terrorism and comply with UN Security Council resolutions 1373, 1390, and 1455. Also calls on states to become a party to all relevant international conventions and protocols relating to terrorism, in particular the 1999 international convention for the suppression of the financing of terrorism.

1.2.13. Security Council Resolution 1526, 2004. Expanded the broad set of measures adopted in resolution 1267 and 1269 (1999). Calls on states to: a) not only freeze the economic resources and financial assets of Al Qaeda connected individuals or groups but also those of "undertakings and entities, including funds derived from property owned or controlled, directly or indirectly by them ... and ensure that neither those funds or any other financial assets ... are made available, directly or indirectly for such person's benefit, by their nationals or by any persons within their territory" and b) move vigorously and decisively to cut the flows of funds and other financial assets and economic resources to individuals and entities associated with the Al Qaeda organization, Osama bin Laden and/or the Taliban, taking into account international codes and standards for combating the financing of terrorism, including those designed to prevent the abuse of nonprofit organizations and informal/alternative remittance systems.

1.2.14. Security Council Resolution 1566, 2004. Recalling that criminal acts, including against civilians, committed with the intent to cause death or serious bodily injury, or taking of hostages, with the purpose to provoke a state of terror, or compel a government or international organization to do or to abstain from doing any act that contravened terrorism-related conventions and protocols, were not justifiable for any reason—whether of a political, philosophical, ideological, racial, ethnic or religious nature. Further, the council established a working group consisting of all its members, which would submit recommendations on practical measures to be imposed on individuals, groups or entities involved in or associated with terrorist activities, other than those designated by the Al Qaeda/Taliban Sanctions Committee. The recommendations could include more effective procedures for bringing the perpetrators to justice through prosecution and extradition.

1.2.15. **Security Council Resolution 1617, 2005.** Extended sanctions against Al Qaeda, Osama bin Laden, and the Taliban, and strengthened previous related resolutions. This resolution extends the mandate of the 1267 Sanctions Committee's Monitoring Team: the eight experts, including one American, who are its eyes and ears. It also clarified what constitutes association with Al Qaeda, adds enhanced due-process provisions to the listing process, and strongly urges all member states to implement the comprehensive international standards embodied in the FATF Forty Recommendations on Money Laundering and the FATF Nine Special Recommendations on Terrorist Financing. In addition, the Council requested the Secretary-General increase cooperation between the UN and INTERPOL in order to provide the 1267 Committee with better tools to fulfill its mandate and urged member states to ensure that stolen and lost passports and other travel documents were invalidated as soon as possible, as well as to share information on those documents with other member states through the INTERPOL database.

1.2.16. **Security Council Resolution 1624, 2005.** Is a resolution related to the incitement of terrorist acts. Calls upon all states to a) cooperate, inter alia, to strengthen the security of their international borders— including by combating fraudulent travel documents and, to the extent attainable, by enhancing terrorist screening and passenger security procedures—and b) continue international efforts to enhance dialogue and broaden understanding among civilizations—in an effort to prevent the indiscriminate targeting of different religions and cultures, and to take all measures as may be necessary and appropriate and in accordance with their obligations under international law to counter incitement of terrorist acts motivated by extremism and intolerance and to prevent the subversion of educational, cultural, and religious institutions by terrorists and their supporters.

1.2.17. Security Council Resolution 1730, 2006. Expanded on UNSCR 1617 and added an element of due process to designation mechanism. UNSCR 1730: a) emphasizes that sanctions are an important tool in the maintenance and restoration of international peace and security; b) adopts delisting procedures and requests the Secretary-General establish within the Secretariat (Security Council Subsidiary Organs Branch), a focal point to receive delisting requests and to perform the tasks described in the annex to UNSCR 1730; and c) directs the sanctions committees established by the Security Council, including those established pursuant to resolution 1718 (2006), 1636 (2005),1591 (2005), 1572 (20040, 1533 (2004), 1521 (2005), 1518 (2003), 1267 (1999), 1132 (1997), 918 (1994), and 751 (1992) to revise their guidelines accordingly

1.2.18. Security Council Resolution 1735, 2006. Is a rollover of UNSCR 1617, reaffirming 1267, 1373, 1617, standardizing listing procedures through use of cover sheet and statement of case. Expresses deep concern about the criminal misuse of the Internet and the nature of the threat in particular the ways in which terrorist ideologies are promoted by Al Qaeda, Osama bin Laden, and the Taliban, and other individuals, groups, undertakings, and entities associated with them, in furtherance of terrorist acts. Freezes the funds and other financial assets or economic resources of these individuals, groups, undertakings and entities, including funds derived from property owned or controlled, directly or indirectly, by them or by persons acting on their behalf or at their direction, and ensure that neither these nor any other funds, financial assets or economic resources are made available, directly or indirectly, for such persons' benefit, or by their nationals or by persons within their territory. In addition it updates some of the procedures and forms for listing and delisting terrorist to the committee for placement on the consolidated list as initially outlined in UNSCR 1267 and 1333.

Authors Note: As of June 2007, the UN had not passed any Security Council resolutions regarding terrorist financing.

1.3. General Assembly Resolutions

1.3.1. General Assembly Resolution 49/60, 1994. Approves the Declaration on Measures to Eliminate International Terrorism, which, among other things, unequivocally condemns all acts of terrorism, demands that states take effective and resolute measures to eliminate terrorism, and charges the Secretary General with various implementation tasks. Some of these tasks include collecting data on the status of existing international agreements relating to terrorism and developing an international legal framework of conventions on terrorism. The first international legal use of the term "terrorist financing" appeared in the UN General Assembly's seminal Declaration on Measures to Eliminate International Terrorism in 1994.

1.3.2. General Assembly Resolution 51/210, 1996. Calls upon states to adopt further measures to prevent and combat terrorism. Some of these include accelerating research and development of explosive detection and marking technology; investigating the abuse of charitable, social, and cultural organizations by terrorist organizations; and developing mutual legal assistance procedures to facilitate cross-border investigations. Further calls upon states to become parties to relevant international antiterrorism conventions and protocols. Also establishes an ad hoc committee to develop an international convention for the suppression of terrorist bombings and acts of nuclear terrorism. Approves a supplement to the 1994 declaration on measures to Eliminate International Terrorism, which, among other things, reaffirms that asylum seekers may not avoid prosecution for terrorist acts and encourages states to facilitate terrorist extraditions even in the absence of a treaty.

1.3.3. **General Assembly Resolution 52/165, 1997.** Reiterates General Assembly Resolution 51/210. Reaffirms the Declaration on Measures to Eliminate International Terrorism. Requests the ad hoc committee established by UN General Assembly Resolution 51/210 continue its work. Requests the Secretary General to invite the International Atomic Energy Agency to assist the ad hoc committee.

1.3.4. **General Assembly Resolutions 53/108, 1999.** Recalls General Assembly Resolution 52/165. Reaffirms that actions by states to combat terrorism should be conducted in conformity with the charter of the UN, international law, and relevant conventions. Decides to address the question of convening a UN conference to formulate a joint response to terrorism by the international community. Decides the ad hoc committee shall continue to elaborate on a draft convention for the suppression of terrorist financing and will continue developing a draft convention for the suppression of acts of nuclear terrorism.

1.3.5. **General Assembly Resolution 54/109, 2000.** Adopts the International Convention for the Suppression of the Financing of Terrorism and urges all states to sign and ratify, accept, approve, or accede to the convention.

1.3.6. **General Assembly Resolution 54/110, 2000.** Notes the establishment of the Terrorism Prevention Branch of the Centre for International Crime Prevention in Vienna, Austria. Invites states to submit information on their national laws, regulations, or initiatives regarding terrorism to the Secretary General.

Invites regional intergovernmental organizations to do likewise. Continues the previous work of the ad hoc committee.

1.3.7. General Assembly Resolution 55/158, 2001. Reiterates General Assembly Resolution 54/110. Welcomes the efforts of the Terrorism Branch of the Centre for International Crime Prevention. Continues the previous work of the ad hoc committee.

1.3.8. General Assembly Resolution 56/88, 2002. Calls upon states to refrain from financing, encouraging, providing training for, or otherwise supporting terrorist activities. Urges all states that have not yet done so to consider, as a matter of priority, and in accordance with Security Council resolution 1373 (2001), becoming parties to relevant conventions and protocols as referred to in paragraph 6 of General Assembly resolution 51/210, as well as become parties to International Convention for the Suppression of the Financing of Terrorism and calls upon all states to enact, as appropriate, domestic legislation necessary to implement the provisions of those conventions and protocols, to ensure that the jurisdiction of their courts enables them to bring to trial the perpetrators of terrorist acts, and to cooperate with and provide support and assistance to other states and relevant international and regional organizations to that end.

1.3.9. General Assembly Resolution 56/288, 2002. Decided to consider further requirements necessary for conference and support servicing of the Counterterrorism Committee in the context of the first performance report at its fifty-seventh session.

1.3.10. General Assembly Resolution 57/27, 2003. Reiterates its call upon states to refrain from financing, encouraging, providing training for, or otherwise supporting terrorist activities. Reiterates General Assembly Resolution 56/88 with regard to terrorist financing.

1.3.11. **General Assembly Resolution 57/219, 2003.** Affirms that states must ensure that any measure taken to combat terrorism complies with their obligations under international law, in particular international human rights, refugee, and humanitarian law. Encourages states, while countering terrorism, to take into account relevant UN resolutions and decisions on human rights and to consider the recommendations of the special procedures and mechanisms of the Commission on Human Rights and the relevant comments and views of UN human rights treaty bodies.

1.3.12. **General Assembly Resolution 58/81, 2004.** Reiterates its call upon states to refrain from financing, encouraging, providing training for or otherwise supporting terrorist activities. Reiterates General Assembly Resolution 56/88 with regard to terrorist financing.

1.3.13. **General Assembly Resolution 58/136, 2004.** Supports the ongoing efforts of the executive director of the UN Office on Drugs and Crime to enhance an integrated approach to combating terrorism, drug trafficking, transnational organized crime, and other related forms of criminal activity. Stresses the need for close coordination and cooperation between states, international, regional, and sub-regional organizations and the Counterterrorism Committee, as well as the Centre for International Crime Prevention, in preventing and combating terrorism and criminal activities carried out for the purpose of furthering terrorism in all its forms and manifestations. Encourages the activities of the Centre for International Crime Prevention of the UN Office on Drugs and Crime within its mandates in the area of preventing terrorism by providing member states, upon request, with technical assistance, specifically to implement the universal conventions and protocols related to terrorism.

1.3.14. General Assembly Resolution 58/174, 2004. Expresses concern about the growing connection between terrorist groups and other criminal organizations engaged in the illegal traffic in arms and drugs at the national and international levels, as well as the consequent commission of serious crimes such as murder, extortion, kidnapping, assault, the taking of hostages, and robbery, and requests the relevant UN bodies to continue to give special attention to this question.

1.3.15. General Assembly Resolution 58/187, 2004. Reiterates General Assembly Resolution 57/219. Notes also the declaration on the issue of combating terrorism contained in the annex to Security Council resolution 1456 (2003), in particular the statement that states must ensure that any measures taken to combat terrorism comply with all their obligations under international law and should adopt such measures in accordance with international law, in particular international human rights, refugee, and humanitarian law.

1.3.16. General Assembly Resolution 59/46, 2004. Reiterates General Assembly Resolution 56/88 with regard to terrorist financing. In addition, urges states to ensure that their nationals or other persons and entities within their territory that willfully provide or collect funds for the benefit of persons or entities who commit, or attempt to commit, facilitate, or participate in the commission of terrorist acts are punished by penalties consistent with the grave nature of such acts.

1.3.17. General Assembly Resolution 59/153, 2005. Reiterates General Assembly Resolution 58/136.

1.3.18. General Assembly Resolution 59/195, 2005. Emphasizes the need to intensify the fight against terrorism at the national level, to enhance effective international cooperation in combating terrorism in conformity with international law, including relevant state obligations under international human rights and international humanitarian law, and to strengthen the role of the UN in this respect. Emphasizes also that states shall deny safe haven to those who finance, plan, support or commit terrorist acts or provide safe havens. States concern with the tendencies to link terrorism and violence with religion and reject the identification of terrorism with any religion, nationality or culture.

1.3.19. **General Assembly Resolution 60/43, 2006.** Reiterates General Assembly Resolution 59/46 with regard to terrorist financing. In addition, urges all states that have not yet done so to consider, as a matter of priority, and in accordance with Security Council resolutions 1373 and 1566, to become parties to International Convention for the Suppression of the Financing of Terrorism.

1.3.20. **General Assembly Resolution 60/288, 2006.** UN Global Counterterrorism Strategy recommends measures to: a) address the conditions conducive to the spread of terrorism; b) prevent and combat terrorism, to include encouraging states to implement the comprehensive international standards embodied in the Forty Recommendations and Nine Special Recommendations of the FATF, recognizing that states may require assistance in implementing them; c) build states' capacity to prevent and combat terrorism and to strengthen the role of the UN system in this regard, to include encouraging IMF, World Bank, UNODC, and INTERPOL to enhance cooperation with states to help them to comply fully with international norms and obligations to combat money-laundering and the terrorist financing; and d) ensure respect for human rights for and the rule of law as the fundamental basis of the fight against terrorism, to include domestic laws and regulations that state any person who participates in the financing, planning, preparation, or perpetration of terrorist acts or in support of terrorist acts is categorized as a serious criminal.

1.3.21. General Assembly Resolution 61/40, 2006. Requests the Terrorism Prevention Branch of the UN Office on Drugs and Crime in Vienna to continue its efforts to enhance, through its mandate, the capabilities of the UN in the prevention of terrorism, and recognizes, in the context of the UN Global Counterterrorism Strategy and Security Council resolution 1373 (2001), its role in assisting states in becoming parties to and implementing the relevant international conventions and protocols relating to terrorism, including the most recent among them, and in strengthening international cooperation mechanisms in criminal matters related to terrorism, including through national capacity building. Reiterates General Assembly Resolution 60/288 with regard to terrorist financing.

Authors Note. As of June 2007, the UN had not passed any general resolutions regarding terrorist financing.

2. INTERPOL
2.1 General Assembly Resolutions
2.1.1. General Assembly Resolution AGN/67/RES/12, 1998. Declared that INTERPOL: a) strongly condemns all terrorist acts, methods, and practices as criminal and unjustifiable; b) supports the proposal to organize, under the aegis of the UN, an international conference on combating terrorism, with the aim of setting up, in close coordination with INTERPOL, a common international strategy for taking all appropriate prevention, protection, surveillance, and law enforcement measures and to prepare concrete proposals for more effective action in combating terrorism, its funding, and support networks; c) supports the idea of implementing an international action plan to strengthen police and judicial cooperation between member countries by eliminating the obstacles which hinder the extradition of fugitive terrorists, the sharing of

158

information, and the adoption of specific criminal charges relating to the use of new technologies for terrorist purposes; and d) feels it is necessary for all members to undertake the principle of international solidarity in the fight against terrorism.

2.1.2. General Assembly Resolution AGN/68/RES/2, 1999.
States that the fight against international terrorism is one of the main aims of INTERPOL's action in carrying out its general activities of police cooperation. Strongly condemns all terrorist acts, methods, and practices as criminal and unjustifiable. Calls upon all INTERPOL member states to refrain from financing, encouraging, or otherwise supporting terrorist activities wherever and by whomever committed them. Supports all efforts to adopt the International Convention for the Suppression of Terrorist Financing at the 54th Session of the UN General Assembly, including the use of INTERPOL as a channel for the exchange of information between law enforcement authorities. Recommended that the National Central Bureaus of member states facilitate the exchange, between their appropriate authorities, of information relating to the financing of terrorism within the framework to be provided by the proposed UN Convention on the Financing of Terrorism.

APPENDIX F. U.S. Laws, Federal Regulations, Federal Register Notices, and Miscellaneous Sources of DoD Authority[1]

(Adapted by the author based on the work of Jeff Breinholt, "Counterterrorism Enforcement: A Lawyer's Guide," Office of Legal Education, 2004, 1-285 and the author's analysis based on government, industry, and various other research sources.)

1. U.S. Laws

A law is a binding custom or practice of a community, a rule of conduct or action prescribed or formally recognized as binding or enforced by a controlling authority. Law implies imposition by a sovereign authority and the obligation of obedience on the part of all subject to that authority.

1.1. United Nations Participation Act (UNPA) of 1945.

Provides the basic authority for U.S. participation as a member of the UN organization. In particular, it is the authority for the President to apply economic and other sanctions against a target country or its nationals pursuant to mandatory decisions by the UN Security Council under Article 41 of the UN Charter. Until recently, this statutory authority was rarely invoked, but in current practice it has become a significant basis for U.S. economic sanctions and the fight against terrorist financing.

1.2. Currency and Foreign Transactions Reporting Act of 1970.

Commonly referred to as the Bank Secrecy Act (BSA) is the basic anti-moneylaundering statutes requiring the reporting of large cash transactions and suspicious financial activities. The BSA requires banks (and now a host of other financial institutions, including broker dealers, credit card companies, insurance companies, and money service businesses) to understand, control, and report transactions that may have a questionable origin or purpose. Specifically, the act requires financial institutions to keep records of cash purchases of negotiable instruments, file reports of cash transactions exceeding $10,000 (daily aggregate amount), and to report suspicious activity that might signify money laundering, tax evasion, or other criminal activities. The Treasury Department has statutory authority to administer the BSA and has delegated this authority to FinCEN.

1.3. International Emergency Economic Powers Act (IEEPA), 1977. Grants the President authority to regulate a comprehensive range of commercial and financial transactions with another country in order to deal with a threat to the national security, foreign policy, or economy of the U.S, if the President declares a national emergency. This has been the basis for economic sanctions since expiration of the Export Administration Act. The IEEPA falls under the provisions of the National Emergencies Act, which means that an emergency declared under the act must be renewed annually to remain in effect, and can be terminated by Congressional legislation.

1.4. Antiterrorism and Effective Death Penalty Act (AEDPA), 1996. Title I amends federal habeas corpus law as it applies to both state and federal prisoners whether on death row or imprisoned for a term of years. Title II expands the circumstances under which foreign governments that support terrorism may be sued for resulting injuries and increases the assistance and compensation available to victims of terrorism. Title III is crafted to help sever international terrorists from their sources of financial and material support. It enlarges the proscriptions against assisting in the commission of various terrorist crimes. It authorizes the regulation of fundraising by foreign organizations associated with terrorist activities. Title V adjusts the restrictions on possession and use of materials capable of producing catastrophic damage in the hands of terrorists. Additionally the act requires U.S. financial institutions in possession or control of funds in which a foreign terrorist organization or its agent has an interest are required to block such funds and report on the funds to the Treasury Department.

1.4.1. **Section 302 of the AEDPA (Title 8 USC, section 1189).** Authorizes the Secretary of State, in consultation with the Secretary of the Treasury and the Attorney General, to designate organizations meeting stated criteria as foreign terrorist organizations, with prior notification to the Congress of the Secretary's intent to designate.

1.4.2. **Section 303 of the AEDPA (Title 18 USC, section 2339B).** Makes it a crime for persons within the U.S. or subject to U.S. jurisdiction to knowingly provide material support or resources to a foreign terrorist organization designated under Section 302.

1.5. **The Money Laundering and Financial Crimes Strategy Act, 1998.** Requires the President, acting through the Secretary of the Treasury and in consultation with the Attorney General and other relevant federal, state, and local law enforcement and regulatory officials to develop and submit an annual National Money Laundering Strategy to the Congress each year from 1999 through 2003. The initial strategy set forth a series of action designed to advance four fundamental goals in the fight against money laundering: a) strengthening domestic enforcement, b) enhancing the measures taken by banks and other financial institutions, c) building stronger partnerships with state and local governments, and d) bolstering international cooperation. The Act also authorized the Secretary of the Treasury to designate High Intensity Money Laundering and Related Financial Crime Areas (HIFCA), in which federal, state, and local law enforcement would work cooperatively to develop a focused and comprehensive approach to targeting money-laundering activity.

1.6. **Uniting and Strengthening America by Providing Appropriate Tools Required to Intercept and Obstruct Terrorism Act (USA Patriot Act), 2001.** Contains tools to enhance the U.S. ability to combat the financing of terrorism and money laundering. Title III of the USA Patriot Act concerns international money laundering abatement and antiterrorism financing. The Patriot Act adds additional burdens on banks and brokerages to report suspicious activities and to compile data on customers, as well as expand forfeiture laws, restrict the ability of shell banks to do business in the U.S., and encourage information exchange between the government and private banks. The private banking industry serves as a front line of investigation regarding terrorist financing.

1.6.1. **USA Patriot Act, Title III, International Money Laundering and Anti-Terrorist Financing Act, 2001.** Supplied Treasury with a host of new and important weapons to both systematically eliminate known risks to the U.S. financial system as well as to identify and nullify new risks that develop.

1.6.2. **USA Patriot Act, Title 31 USC, section 5332, Bulk Cash Smuggling.** Makes it a crime to smuggle or attempt to smuggle over $10,000 in currency or monetary instruments into or out of the U.S., with the specific intent to evade the U.S. currency-reporting requirements codified at 31 USC 5316.

1.6.3. **USA Patriot Act, section 311.** Provides the Secretary of the Treasury with authority to require U.S. financial institutions to apply graduated, proportionate countermeasures against a foreign jurisdiction, a foreign financial institution, a type of international transaction, or a type of account that the Secretary finds to be a "primary money laundering concern." It also added a new section, 5318A, to the BSA.

1.6.4. **USA Patriot Act, section 312.** Requires U.S. financial institutions that establish, maintain, administer, or manage a "private banking account" or a correspondent account for a non-U.S. person (including a foreign bank) to apply due diligence, and in some cases enhanced due diligence, procedures, and controls to detect and report instances of money laundering through those accounts.

1.6.5. USA Patriot Act, section 313. Prohibits U.S. banks, securities brokers, and dealers from maintaining correspondent accounts for foreign shell banks, that is, unregulated banks with no physical presence in any jurisdiction. Also requires financial institutions to take reasonable steps to ensure that foreign banks with correspondent accounts do not themselves permit access to such accounts by foreign shell banks. Adds subsection (j) to 31 USC section 5318 to prohibit depository institutions and securities brokers and dealers operating in the U.S. from establishing, maintaining, administering, or managing correspondent accounts for foreign shell banks, other than shell bank vehicles affiliated with recognized and regulated depository institutions.

1.6.6. USA Patriot Act, section 314(a). Encourages cooperation and the sharing of information relating to money laundering and terrorism among law enforcement authorities, regulatory authorities, and financial institutions

1.6.7. USA Patriot Act, section 314 (b). Upon notice to the Secretary of the Treasury, permits the sharing among financial institutions of information relating to individuals, entities, organizations, and countries suspected of possible terrorist or money laundering activities.

1.6.8. USA Patriot Act, section 318. Expands the definition of financial institutions for purposes of 18 USC section 1956 and 1957 to include those operating outside the U.S.

1.6.9. **USA Patriot Act, section 319(b).** Amended asset forfeiture law (18 USC section 981) and authorizes the Secretary of the Treasury or the Attorney General to issue a summons or subpoena to any foreign bank that maintains a correspondent account in the U.S. requesting records relating to that correspondent account. Requires U.S. financial institutions that maintain a correspondent account for a foreign bank to keep records identifying a) the owners of the foreign bank and b) the name and address of a person in the U.S. who is authorized to accept service of legal process for records related to the correspondent account.

1.6.10. **USA Patriot Act, section 324.** Requires the Secretary of the Treasury, in consultation with the Attorney General and the federal functional regulators, to evaluate the operations of Title III and submit recommendations for legislative amendments that may be necessary.

1.6.11. **USA Patriot Act, section 325.** Authorizes the Secretary of the Treasury to issue regulations concerning the maintenance of concentration accounts by U.S. depository institutions to ensure such accounts are not used to prevent association of the identity of an individual customer with the movement of funds of which the customer is the direct or beneficial owner.

1.6.12. **USA Patriot Act, section 326(a).** Requires the Secretary of the Treasury to promulgate minimum standards for financial institutions and their customers regarding the identity of the customer that must apply in connection with the opening of an account at a financial institution. The minimum standards must require financial institutions to implement, and customers (after being given adequate notice) to comply with, reasonable procedures concerning verification of customer identity, maintenance of records for identity verification, and consultation at account opening of lists of known or suspect terrorists provided by a financial institution by a government agency.

1.6.13. **USA Patriot Act, section 326(b).** Requires the Secretary of the Treasury, in consultation with the federal functional regulators (as well as other appropriate agencies), to submit a report to Congress within six months of the date of enactment containing recommendations about the most effective way to require foreign nationals to provide financial institutions in the U.S. with accurate identity information comparable to that required to be provided by U.S. nationals, and to obtain an identification number that would function similarly to a U.S. national's Social Security or tax identification number.

1.6.14. **USA Patriot Act, section 328.** Requires the Secretary of the Treasury, in consultation with the Attorney General and the Secretary of State, to take reasonable steps to encourage foreign governments to include originator information in wire transfer instructions.

1.6.15. **USA Patriot Act, section 352.** Requires anti-money-laundering programs, for all financial institutions.

1.6.16. **USA Patriot Act, section 356(a).** Directs the Secretary of the Treasury, in consultation with the Securities and Exchange Commission and the Board of Governors of the Federal Reserve, to prescribe regulations requiring securities broker-dealers to file suspicious activity reports to the extent considered necessary and expedient.

1.6.17. **USA Patriot Act, section 356 (b).** Authorizes the Secretary, in consultation with the Commodity Futures Trading Commission, to prescribe regulations requiring futures commission merchants, commodity trading advisors, and commodity pool operators to file suspicious activity reports.

1.6.18. **USA Patriot Act, section 356 (c).** Requires the Secretary of the Treasury, the Board of Governors of the Federal Reserve, and the Securities and Exchange Commission to submit jointly a report to Congress recommending ways to apply BSA requirements to investment companies.

1.6.19. **USA Patriot Act, section 357.** Requires the Secretary of the Treasury to submit a report to Congress on the role of the Internal Revenue Service (IRS) in the administration of the BSA.

1.6.20. **USA Patriot Act, section 358.** Expanded Treasury's ability to share BSA information with the intelligence community, clarified that the Right to Financial Privacy Act does not preclude the use of financial information to combat international terrorism, and gave law enforcement and intelligence agencies access to credit reports when the inquiry relates to international terrorism.

1.6.21. **USA Patriot Act, section 359.** Requires the Secretary of the Treasury to submit a report on the need for additional legislation relating to Agricultural Research Service. Clarifies that the BSA treats certain underground banking systems and money transmitting businesses as financial institutions for purposes of the funds transfer record-keeping and other anti-money-laundering rules. The Secretary of the Treasury must report to Congress by October 26, 2002 on the need for additional legislation or regulatory controls relating to underground banking systems.

1.6.22. **USA Patriot Act, section 360.** Authorizes the Secretary of the Treasury to instruct the U.S. executive director of each international financial institution to use such Directors' "voice and vote" to support loans and other use of resources to benefit nations that the President determines are contributing to U.S.

efforts to combat international terrorism, and to require the periodic auditing of disbursements at such international financial institutions to ensure that funds are not paid to persons engaged in or supporting terrorism.

1.6.23. **USA Patriot Act, section 361.** Requires, to the extent considered necessary and expedient, the Secretary of the Treasury to submit a report on improving compliance with the reporting (Report of Foreign Bank and Financial Accounts) requirements of section 5314 of Title 31, United States Code (USC).

1.6.24. **USA Patriot Act, section 362.** Requires the Secretary of the Treasury to establish a highly secure network within FinCEN for filing of BSA reports.

1.6.25. **USA Patriot Act, section 365.** Requires nonfinancial trades or businesses to file currency transaction reports with FinCEN. Provides Treasury and law enforcement with access to currency reports filed by nonfinancial trades or businesses, a form previously difficult to obtain in light of IRS confidentiality restrictions.

1.6.26. **USA Patriot Act, section 366.** Requires, to the extent considered necessary and expedient, the Secretary of the Treasury to report to Congress on whether to expand the existing exemptions to the requirement that financial institutions file currency transaction reports and on methods for improving financial institution utilization of exemptions.

1.6.27. **USA Patriot Act, section 371.** Addresses the known risks associated with the smuggling of bulk cash and currency by making it an offense under Title 31 not to declare amounts in excess of $10,000 to the Customs Service.

1.6.28. **USA Patriot Act, section 373.** Amended 18 USC section 1960 to prohibit unlicensed money services businesses. In addition, such businesses must file suspicious activity reports with law enforcement officials.

1.6.29. **USA Patriot Act, section 377.** Provides extraterritorial jurisdiction for the financial crimes committed abroad where the tools or proceeds of the offense pass through or are in the U.S. (example given, the account issuer or credit card system).

1.6.30. **USA Patriot Act, section 411.** U.S. persons are prohibited from having dealings and must block the assets within U.S. jurisdiction of terrorists and terrorist groups that are designated by the Departments of State and Treasury, and those who are owned or controlled by, acting for or on behalf of, or materially, financially, or technologically assisting designated terrorists, terrorist groups, or their supporters.

1.7. **Terrorism Risk Insurance Act (TRIA), 2002.** Establishes a temporary federal program of shared public and private compensation for insured commercial property and casualty losses resulting from acts of terrorism covered by TRIA. The intent of TRIA was to stimulate business investment that had slowed to a trickle after the events of 11 September 2001. The law creates a three-year federal program that backs up insurance companies and guarantees that certain terrorist-related claims will be paid. On 22 December 2005, President Bush signed into law the Terrorism Risk Insurance Extension Act of 2005, which extends TRIA through 31 December 2007.

1.8. **Intelligence Reform and Terrorism Prevention Act (IRTPA), 2004.** IRTPA consists of eight separate titles that address topics of vital interest to terrorism prosecutors and others engaged on the legal front of the war on terror. These topics include: a) reform of the intelligence community; b) improvements in the intelligence capabilities of the FBI; c) revamping and uniformity of security clearance procedures; measures to enhance transportation security; d) improvements in border protection; e) immigration and visa procedures; f) new tools for terrorism prosecutors; implementation of 9/11 Commission Recommendations; g) establishment of interagency mechanisms concerning information and intelligence sharing, infrastructure protection and analysis, and civil rights and civil liberties; and h) established both the position of DNI and the NCTC.

1.9. Combating Terrorism Financing Act, 2005. Has been brought to Congress two times but has never become law. Would amend: a) the International Emergency Economic Powers Act to increase penalties for violating a license, order, or regulation under the Act; b) the Racketeer Influenced and Corrupt Organizations Act (RICO) to expand its scope to include offenses relating to the financing of terrorism and violations of the Social Security Act relating to obtaining funds through the misuse of a Social Security number; c) the federal criminal code to: (i) provide for civil forfeiture to the U.S. of the assets of any individual or organization engaged in planning or perpetrating an act of international terrorism against any international organization or foreign government and (ii) establish procedures for contesting the confiscation of assets of suspected international terrorists; and d) RICO to make receiving military-type training from a foreign terrorist organization a predicate offense to violation of money laundering provisions. Authorizes DHS to investigate violations of money laundering and related offenses.

1.10. Foreign Intelligence Surveillance Act (FISA), 1978. Was passed to produce legal guidelines for federal investigations of foreign intelligence targets. Among the rules put in place were regulations governing: a) electronic surveillance, b) physical searches, c) pen registers and trap and trace devices for foreign intelligence purposes, and d) access to certain business records for foreign intelligence purposes. In addition to defining how foreign intelligence investigations were to be performed, FISA also defined who could be investigated. Only foreign powers or agents of foreign powers were to be subject to FISA investigations. Thus, targets are primarily those foreign persons who are engaged in espionage or international terrorism.

1.11. Public Law 102-138 section 304 as amended by Public Law 103-236 (22 USC section 2656g). Requires Treasury to submit the Terrorist Assets Reports to the Committee on Foreign Relations and the Committee on Finance of the Senate and to the Committee on International Relations and the Committee on Ways and Means of the House.

2. Federal Regulations

Rules or orders issued by an executive authority or regulatory agency of a government and having the force of law.

2.1. United States Code (USC). Is the codification by subject matter of the general and permanent laws of the U.S. It is divided by broad subjects into 50 titles and published by the Office of the Law Revision Counsel of the U.S. House of Representatives. Since 1926, the USC has been published every six years. In between editions, annual cumulative supplements are published in order to present the most current information. USC are laws made by the U.S. Congress.

2.1.1. Title 18 USC section 1956. Makes it illegal to: a) conduct or attempt to conduct a financial transaction with proceeds known to be from specified unlawful activity, b) transport or attempt to transport monetary instruments or funds to or from the U.S., and c) conduct or attempt to conduct a financial transaction involving property a law enforcement officer represents to be the proceeds of specified unlawful activity or property used to conduct or facilitate specified unlawful activity. The criminalization of money laundering was largely in response to the massive amounts of money exchanging hands and sifting through American financial institutions as a product of the illegal trade of narcotics. Clearly, with the Patriot Act's amplified reporting and due diligence requirements, Congress has intended to provide a means to conduct additional financial analysis as part of a counterterrorist financing regime.

2.1.2. Title 18 USC section 1957. Makes it illegal knowingly to engage or attempt to engage in a monetary transaction involving property valued at more than $10,000 if it is derived from specified unlawful activity.

2.1.3. Title 18 USC section 2331(1). The term *international terrorism* means activities that: a) involve violent acts or acts dangerous to human life that are a violation of the criminal laws of the U.S or of any state, or that would be a criminal violation if committed within the jurisdiction of the U.S or of any state; b) appear to be intended: (i) to intimidate or coerce a civilian population; (ii) to influence the policy of a government by intimidation or coercion; or (iii) to affect the conduct of a government by mass destruction, assassination, or kidnapping; and c) occur primarily outside the territorial jurisdiction of the U.S. or transcend national boundaries in terms of the means by which they are accomplished, the persons they appear intended to intimidate or coerce, or the locale in which their perpetrators operate or seek asylum.

2.1.4. Title 18 USC section 2331(5). The term "domestic terrorism" means activities that: a) involve acts dangerous to human life that are a violation of the criminal laws of the U.S. or of any state; b) appear to be intended to: (i) intimidate or coerce a civilian population; (ii) influence the policy of a government by intimidation or coercion; or (iii) affect the conduct of a government by mass destruction, assassination, or kidnapping; and c) occur primarily within the territorial jurisdiction of the U.S.

2.1.5. **Title 18 USC section 2339A.** Generally used in conjunction with 18 USC section 1956, section 2339A pertains to providing material support or resources for acts of international terrorism (conspiracies within the United States to kill/maim persons and destroy specific property abroad).

2.1.6. **Title 18 USC section 2339B.** States whoever knowingly provides material support or resources to a foreign terrorist organization, or attempts or conspires to do so, shall be fined under this title or imprisoned not more than 15 years, or both, and, if the death of any person results, shall be imprisoned for any term of years or for life. Except as authorized by the Secretary, any financial institution that becomes aware that it has possession of, or control over, any funds in which a foreign terrorist organization, or its agent, has an interest, shall: a) retain possession of, or maintain control over, such funds and b) report to the Secretary the existence of such funds in accordance with regulations issued by the Secretary. Generally used in conjunction with 18 USC section 1956.

2.1.7. **Title 22 USC section 2656f(d).** The term 'terrorism' means premeditated, politically motivated violence perpetrated against noncombatant targets by subnational groups or clandestine agents, usually intended to influence an audience.

2.1.8. **Title 31 USC section 5318 (k).** Was codified by section 319(b) of the USA Patriot Act, states any covered financial institution that maintains a correspondent account in the U.S. for a foreign bank must maintain records in the U.S. identifying: a) the owner(s) of such foreign bank and b) the name and address of a person (as defined in 31 Code of Federal Regulation section 103.11(z)) who resides in the U.S. and is authorized to accept service of legal process for records concerning the correspondent account.

2.2. **Code of Federal Regulations (C.F.R.).** Is the codification of the general and permanent rules published in the federal regulations. by the executive departments and agencies of the USG. It is divided into 50 titles that represent broad areas subject to federal regulation. Each volume of the C.F.R. is updated once each calendar year and is issued on a quarterly basis.

2.2.1. **31 C.F.R., Chapter 5, Part 594.** Covers various Global Terrorism Sanctions Regulations (Part 594.101–594.901) from relation of this part to other laws and regulations to paperwork reduction act notice.

2.2.2. **31 C.F.R., Chapter 5, Part 595.** Covers various Terrorism Sanctions Regulations (Subpart A (595.101)–Subpart I (595.901)) from relation of this part to other laws and regulations to Paperwork Reduction Act notice.

2.2.3. **31 C.F.R., Chapter 5, Part 596.** Covers various Terrorism List Governments Sanctions Regulations (Subpart A (596.101)–Subpart I (596.901)) from relation of this part to other laws and regulations to Paperwork Reduction Act notice.

2.2.4. **31 C.F.R., Chapter 5, Part 597.** Covers various Foreign Terrorist Organizations Sanctions Regulations (Subpart A (597.101)–Subpart I (597.901)) from relation of this part to other laws and regulations to Paperwork Reduction Act notice.

2.3. **Executive Orders (EOs).** Most EOs are issued by the President to U.S. executive officers to help direct their operation, with the result of failing to comply being removal from office. Some orders do have the force of law when made in pursuance of certain Acts of Congress due to those acts giving the President discretionary powers. Other types of EOs are: a) National Security Directives, b) Homeland Security Presidential Directives, and c) Presidential Decision Directives, which deal with national security and defense matters.

2.3.1. **EO 12947, 1995.** Prohibits transactions with terrorists who threaten to disrupt the Middle East Peace Process. Prohibits transfers, including donations of funds, goods, or services, to any organization or individual designated under its authority and blocks all property in the U.S. or within the possession or control of a U.S. person in which there is an interest of any designated person. Twelve terrorist organizations were named in the Annex to E.O. 12947.

2.3.2. **EO 13099, 1998.** Prohibits transactions with terrorists who threaten to disrupt the Middle East Peace Process (Tab 6), to amend EO 12947 by adding three individuals and one organization to the Annex of EO 12947, including Osama bin Muhammad bin Awad bin Laden (also known as Osama bin Laden) and Al Qaeda.

2.3.3. **EO 13129, 1999.** States that the actions and policies of the Taliban in Afghanistan, in allowing territory under its control in Afghanistan to be used as a safe haven and base of operations for Osama bin Laden and the Al Qaeda organization who have committed and threaten to continue to commit acts of violence against the U.S. and its nationals, constitute an unusual and extraordinary threat to the national security and foreign policy of the U.S., and declared a national emergency to deal with that threat.

2.3.4. **EO 13224, 2001.** Designation under this order results in asset-blocking and a prohibition on transactions with the designated individual or entity. This EO expands the U.S. power to target the support structure of terrorist organizations, freeze the U.S. assets and block the U.S. transactions of terrorists and those that support them, and increases the ability to block U.S. assets of, and deny access to U.S. markets to, foreign banks who refuse to cooperate with U.S. authorities to identify and freeze terrorist assets abroad. This order directed the Secretary of the Treasury, in consultation with the Secretary of State and the Attorney General, to deny financing and financial services to terrorists and terrorist organizations. The executive order authorizes the blocking of assets of those designated individuals and organizations linked to global terrorism. It also prohibits transactions with designated terrorist groups, leaders, and corporate and charitable fronts.

2.3.5. **EO 13268, 2002.** States that the situation that gave rise to the declaration of a national emergency in EO 13129, with respect to the Taliban, in allowing territory under its control in Afghanistan to be used as a safe haven and base of operations for Osama bin Laden and the Al Qaeda organization, has been significantly altered, thus allowing the revocation of EO 13129 and terminating the national emergency declared in that order with respect to the Taliban. In addition it amends section 1 of EO 13224 by including the name of Mohammed Omar.

2.3.6. **EO 13372, 2005.** Clarifies the steps taken in EO 12947 with respect to the implementation of section 203(b)(2) of IEEPA. Amends section 4 of EO 13224 to state that it prohibit donations as provided by section 1 of EO 12947 and that the Trade Sanctions Reform and Export Enhancement Act of 2000 shall not affect the imposition or the continuation of the imposition of any unilateral agricultural sanction or unilateral medical sanction on any person determined to be subject to this order.

3. Federal Register Notices (FRs)
Published by the Office of the Federal Register, National Archives and Records Administration (NARA), the Federal Register is the official daily publication for rules, proposed

rules, and notices of federal agencies and organizations, as well as EOs and other presidential documents.

3.1. **71 FR 27199-06, 2006.** Covers the Treasury Department's, Office of Foreign Assets Control (OFAC) revisions to the Global Terrorism Sanctions Regulations, the Terrorism Sanctions Regulations, and the Foreign Terrorist Organizations Sanctions Regulations to add general licenses authorizing certain transactions with the Palestinian Authority (PA).

3.2. **71 FR 29251-06, 2006.** Covers the Treasury Department's, OFAC revisions to its regulations in order to reflect amendments to the International Emergency Economic Powers Act (IEEPA) made by the Combating Terrorism Financing Act of 2005.

3.3. **71 FR 58742-06, 2006.** Covers OFAC of the U.S. Department of the Treasury revisions to the Global Terrorism Sanctions Regulations, the Terrorism Sanctions Regulations, and the Foreign Terrorist Organizations Sanctions Regulations to authorize in kind donations of medical devices and medical services by U.S. nongovernmental organizations to the PA Ministry of Health.

4. Miscellaneous Sources of DoD Authority

As stated in Chapter 1, currently DoD has no defined authorities under U.S. law and regulations nor does DoD have an overarching policy that supports threat finance. However, DoD derives its roles and responsibilities from the following strategies, plans, execution orders, and assessments.

4.1. **National Strategy for Combating Terrorism (NSCT), 2006.** Builds directly from the National Security Strategy issued in March 2006 as well as the 2003 National Strategy for Combating Terrorism. It focuses on: a) advancing effective democracies as the long-term antidote to the ideology of terrorism, b) preventing attacks by terrorist networks, c) denying weapons of mass destruction to rogue states and terrorist allies, d) denying terrorists the support and sanctuary of rogue states, e) denying terrorists control of any nation they would use as a base or launching pad, and f) laying the foundations and building the institutions and structures the U.S. needs to carry the fight forward against terror. With regard to disrupting terrorist financing it focuses on cutting off individuals and institutions from the networks they depend on for support and that facilitate their activities, and it acknowledges that the effective disruption of funding sources, interdiction of transfer mechanisms, and strengthening allies can help the U.S. and its partners starve terrorist networks of the material support they require.

4.2. **National Military Strategic Plan for the War on Terrorism (NMSP-WOT), 2006.** Constitutes the comprehensive unified military plan to prosecute the Global War on Terrorism for the Armed Forces of the United States ... including the findings and recommendations of the 9/11 Commission and a rigorous examination within the DoD. The plan emphasizes "encouraging" and "enabling" foreign partners, especially in countries where the U.S. is not at war and concludes that the conflict cannot be fought by military means alone—or by the U.S. acting alone. The plan formally directs military commanders to go after a list of eight pressure points at which terrorist groups could be vulnerable: ideological support, weapons, funds, communications and movement, safe havens, foot soldiers, access to targets, and leadership. The plan's No. 1 stated objective is to deny terrorists the resources they need to operate and survive and identifies resources as a critical requirement for terrorist organizations.

4.3. **National Implementation Plan (NIP).** Classified
4.4. **Global War On Terrorism Campaign Plan.** Classified

4.5. **Joint Intelligence Operations Center Execution Order.** Classified

4.6. **Global War on Terrorism Assessment June 05 MSO-1.** Classified

4.7. **National Action Plan for Foreign Fights.** Classified

4.8. **Disrupting External Funding to the Taliban (DEFT).** Classified

4.9. **Moving from Terrorist Finance to Threat Finance.** Classified

4.10. **Terrorist Finance Sub-CSG TIFWG.** Classified

APPENDIX G: Worldwide Information and Intelligence Network (WIIN)

One of the keys to success in the effort to disrupt terrorist organizations is the ability of IA, law enforcement, private sector, allies, and partner nations to conduct integrated and collaborative efforts over a network, such as the proposed WIIN, which is secure, flexible, and allows for timely passage of information, while being robust enough to meet evolving command, control, communications, and computer requirements. While the author is providing an example architecture (WIIN) to facilitate his recommendation, in the end it is not the exact architecture that matters. What is important, however, is establishing a collaborative and integrated network that is predicated on a *need to share* mind set.

The WIIN would provide the following base capabilities at all nodes: a) file sharing and transfer. b) e-mail. c) Web-conferencing using voice over Internet protocol. and d) chat/instant messaging. To support WIIN, a comprehensive Web-based information management (IM) system would need to be developed and maintained by a U.S. central management authority. The IM system would allow information to be published and compartmentalized as required. In addition, the network would provide a clear understanding of the enemy threat through a Common Operating Picture (COP).

All communication systems used in WIIN would comply with National Security Agency (NSA) and Communications Security Establishment (CSE) standards for Type 1 encryption. Contingency electronic KEYMAT fills could be generated and prepared for use with allies and partner nation activities.

Network Architecture

Initially, WIIN would provide a common command and control network available to IA, law enforcement, private sector, allies, and partner nations complementing existing national networks. As WIIN evolves, it would become the common link to optimize network resources and information sharing. The network would support both fixed sites and deployable elements. A transit case communications package would be designed to support deployable elements. The Internet would be used as the transport backbone, and all traffic from site to site would be encrypted in accordance with National Security Agency (NSA) guidelines using Type 1 encryption devices.[159]

Server Enclave. All network services, except Domain Name Service (DNS) and Windows Internet Naming Service (WINS), would be centralized at the server enclave. Server virtualization would be incorporated to reduce the rack space, power, and HVAC (heating, ventilation, and air conditioning) footprints. An emission control (EMC) fiber channel Storage Area Network (SAN) would be used for data storage. The server enclave would have connectivity to the Internet via two 10 Mbps Internet Protocol (IP) connections.

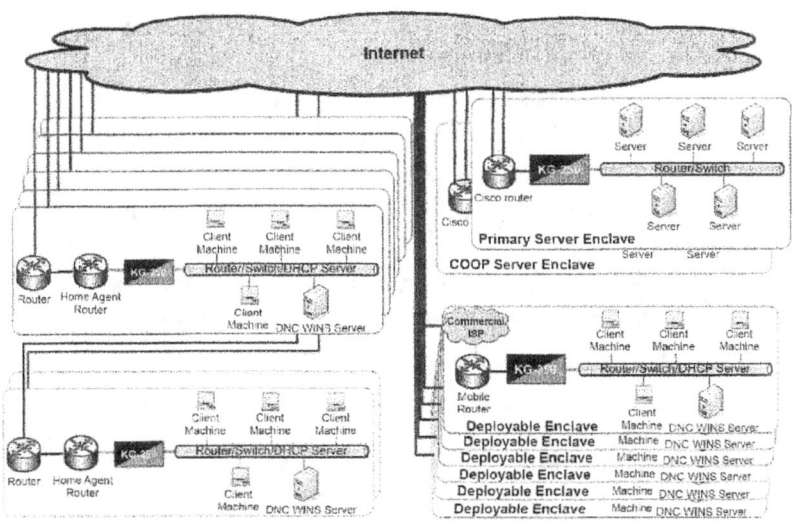

Figure G-1. Network Topology

181

Fixed Site Enclave. Each fixed site would consist of client machines and one DNS/WINS server connected via fiber to an Ethernet switch/Dynamic Host Configuration Protocol (DHCP) server. The switch is connected to the red side of the KG-250. The black side of the KG-250 is connected to a Cisco 3251 Home Agent router. The Home Agent router is connected to another Cisco router. Finally, the Cisco router is connected to the Internet via commercial carrier. The red side of each fixed site would be assigned its own class C network of IP addresses.

Deployable Enclave. Deployable enclaves must have the ability/flexibility to connect to the Internet in several different ways. They must be able to connect via a standard Internet service provider (ISP), or if there is no ISP available, they must be able to access the Internet via other means, such as INMARSAT or satellite communications (SATCOM) connection. The concept of operations for the deployed element incorporates the use of mobile routers. Mobile routers allow the deployed element to operate identically in garrison and deployed environments. There are several advantages to this. It simplifies the setup and configuration of the workstations, since they use the same setup in garrison and deployed. It also allows the computers to continue to be connected to the network when not deployed to receive required patches and updates. This ensures that the machines are fully functional when deployed. The mobile router receives an IP address from an ISP or other provider, then translates that into the static IP range used on the internal side of the network. The mobile router requires the addition of a host-agent router at the fixed site. The host agent acts as an edge router, directing traffic to the mobile users and receiving and verifying information coming from the mobile router before sending it to the crypto equipment for decryption.

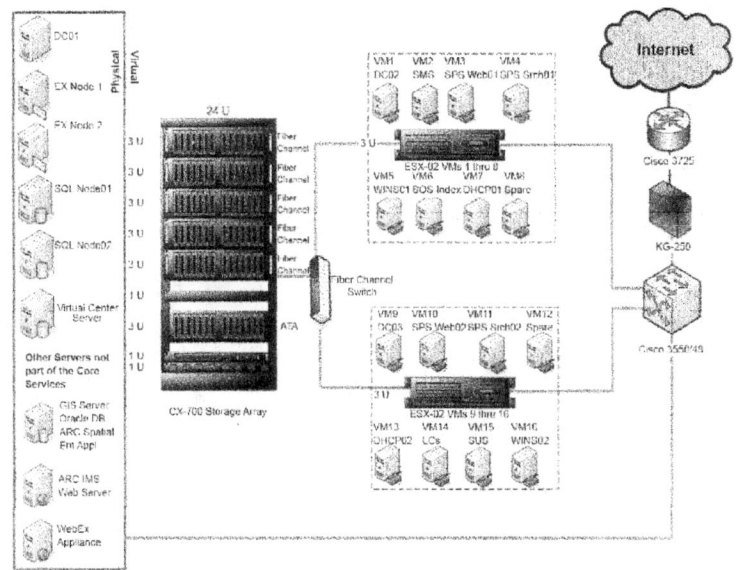

Figure G-2. Server Enclave

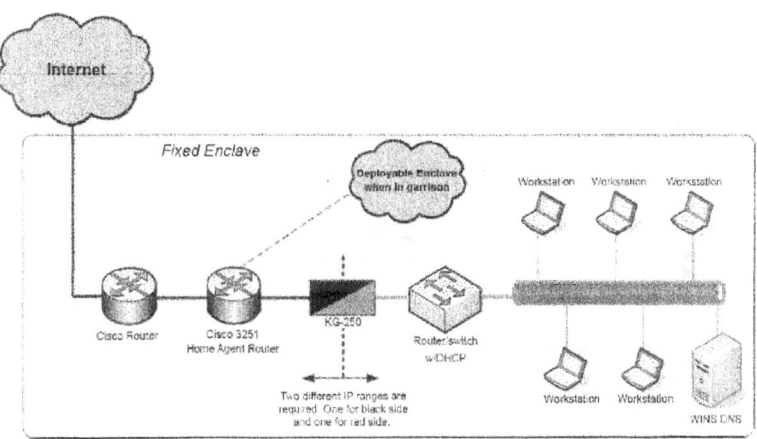

Figure G-3. Fixed Site Enclave

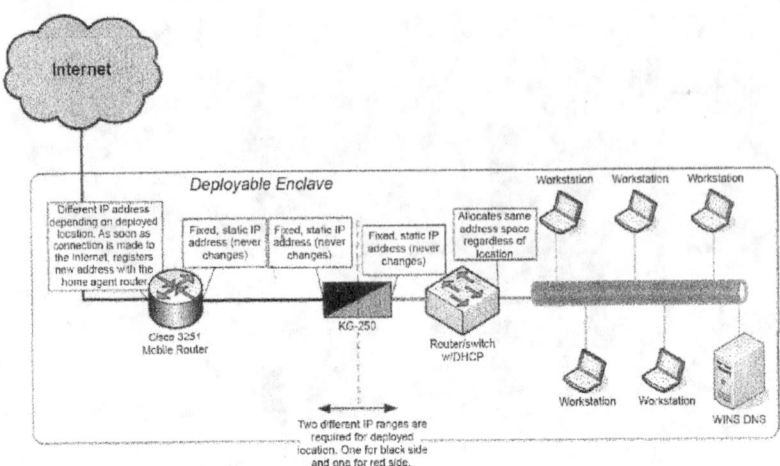

Figure G-4. Deployable Enclave with Direct Internet Connection

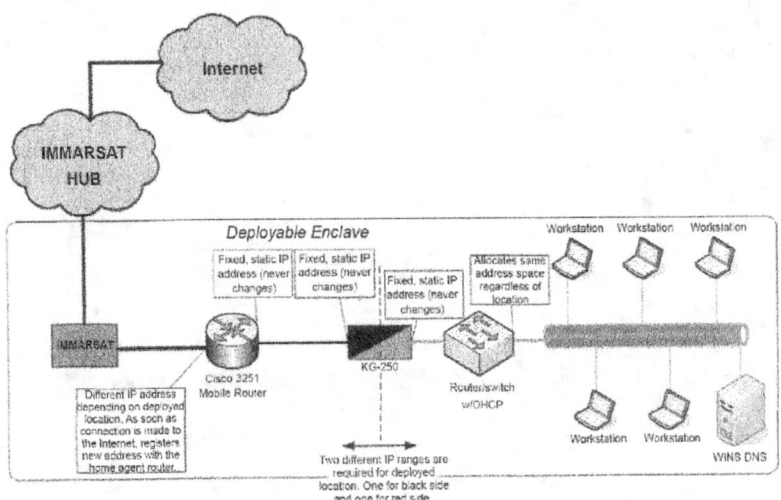

Figure G-5. Deployable Enclave with INMARSAT Connection

Network Services Architecture. All network services would be Web-based and secure sockets layer (SSL)-enabled originating from a centralized location. Because all services are Web-based, there is no need for the machines in the enclaves to

184

be part of the active-directory domain. This reduces the amount of traffic (machines do not have to authenticate to the directory), thereby giving more bandwidth to user-required application data. This architecture also requires very little systems administration support at user enclaves. Both the Primary and Continuity of Operations (COOP) enclaves take advantage of server virtualization to reduce power, cooling, and the physical footprint of the servers.

APPENDIX H. Acronyms and Terms

Acronyms
AML....... Anti-Money Laundering
CIA........ Central Intelligence Agency
CSA........ Combat Support Agencies
CSG....... Counterterrorism Security Group, NSC
DHS....... Department of Homeland Security
DoD........ Department of Defense
DoJ........... Department of Justice
DoS.......... Department of State
EO............ Executive Order
FATF....... Financial Action Task Force
FBI......... Federal Bureau of Investigation
FinCEN.... Financial Crimes Enforcement Network, Treasury Department
FIU.......... Financial Intelligence Unit
FTO......... Foreign Terrorist Organizations
GWOT..... Global War on Terrorism
IC............. Intelligence community
IEEPA. International Emergency Economic Powers Act
ILEA.... International Law Enforcement Agency
IMF......... International Monetary Fund
INL..... The Bureau of International Narcotics and Law Enforcement
Affairs, DoS
INTERPOL The International Criminal Police Organization
JTTF.......... Joint Terrorism Task Force
NCTC. National Counterterrorism Center, IA, ODNI
NSC......... National Security Council
S/CT.. The Office of the Coordinator for Counterterrorism, DoS
TFEU.... Threat Financing Exploitation Unit, DoD
USC......... United States Code

USG........ United States Government
WMD/E. Weapons of Mass Destruction/Effects

TERMS

Bayat. An oath of allegiance to an emir.

Chain or Line Networks. Are simple structures, often used, for example, by smugglers. Information or goods move in a linear direction from one node to the next. Each contact knows his or her next contact, but can identify no one beyond that next contact.

Combating Terrorism. Defined by NMSP-WOT as actions, including antiterrorism (defensive measures taken to reduce vulnerability to terrorist acts) and counterterrorism (offensive measures taken to prevent, deter, and respond to terrorism), taken to oppose terrorism throughout the entire threat spectrum.

Deter. Defined by NMSP-WOT as actions taken to disrupt, prevent, or preclude acts of aggression. Deter includes preemptive actions to unhinge the ability to conduct operations.

Disrupt. Defined by NMSP-WOT as actions taken to interrupt, temporarily prevent, or desynchronize a terrorist network's capability to conduct operations.

Full Matrix Network. Is the most highly-developed network based on the fact that all of its members are connected to, and can communicate with, all other members.

Hawala. A means outside of traditional banking for moving money across borders.

Informal Value Transfer. Any system or network of people facilitating, on a full-time or part-time basis, the transfer of value domestically or internationally outside the conventional, regulated financial institutional systems.

Mitigate. To cause to become less harsh or hostile, to make less severe or painful. In relation to an effect, mitigate means to lessen or eliminate the severity or incidence of an effect.

Money Service Business. Has been defined by FinCEN as check cashers, traveler's check sellers, currency exchangers, stored value sellers, and money transmitters.

String. A sequentially ordered set of things or events or ideas in which each successive member is related to the preceding members; "a string of islands," "train of mourners," "a train of thought."

Terrorist Financing. Is defined as the financial support, in any form, of terrorism or of those who encourage, plan, or engage in it.

Joint Special Operations University and the Strategic Studies Department

The Joint Special Operations University (JSOU) provides its publications to contribute toward expanding the body of knowledge about joint special operations. JSOU publications advance the insights and recommendations of national security professionals and the Special Operations Forces (SOF) students and leaders for consideration by the SOF community and defense leadership.

JSOU is a subordinate organization of the United States Special Operations Command (USSOCOM), MacDill Air Force Base, Florida. The JSOU mission is to educate SOF executive, senior, and intermediate leaders and selected other national and international security decision makers, both military and civilian, through teaching, outreach, and research in the science and art of joint special operations. JSOU provides education to the men and women of SOF and to those who enable the SOF mission in a joint environment.

JSOU conducts research through its Strategic Studies Department where effort centers upon the USSOCOM mission and the commander's priorities.

Mission. Provide fully capable special operations forces to defend the United States and its interests. Plan and synchronize operations against terrorist networks.

Priorities. • Deter, disrupt, and defeat terrorist threats.
• Develop and support our people and their families.
• Sustain and modernize the force.

The Strategic Studies Department also provides teaching and curriculum support to Professional Military Education institutions, the staff colleges and war colleges. It advances SOF strategic influence by its interaction in academic, interagency, and United States military communities.

Joint Special Operations University

Brian A. Maher, Ed.D., Education, *President*
Lieutenant Colonel Michael C. McMahon, *Strategic Studies Department Director*
Colonel (USA, Ret.) William W. Mendel, Colonel (USA, Ret.) Jeffrey W. Nelson, Colonel (USAF, Ret.) Kenneth H. Poole, Captain (USN, Ret.) William S. Wildrick, *Resident Senior Fellows*

Editorial Advisory Board

John B. Alexander, Ph.D., Education, *The Apollinaire Group and JSOU Senior Fellow*

Joseph D. CeleskiColonel, U.S. Army, Ret.*JSOU Senior Fellow*

Chuck CunninghamLieutenant General, U.S. Air Force, Ret., *Professor of Strategy, Joint Advanced Warfighting School and JSOU Associate Fellow*

Gilbert E. DoanMajor, U.S. Army, Ret., *JSOU Institutional Integration Division Chief*

Thomas H. HenriksenPh.D., History, *Hoover Institution Stanford University and JSOU Senior Fellow*

Russell D. HowardBrigadier General, U.S. Army, Ret.*Director of the Jebsen Center for Counter-Terrorism Studies, The Fletcher School, Tufts University and JSOU Senior Fellow*

John D. JogerstColonel, U.S. Air Force, Ret. *18th USAFSOS Commandant*

James KirasPh.D., History, *School of Advanced Air and Space Studies and JSOU Associate Fellow*

Alvaro de Souza PinheiroMajor General, Brazilian Army, Ret.*JSOU Associate Fellow*

James F. Powers, Jr.Colonel, U.S. Army, Ret.*Director of Homeland Security, Commonwealth of Pennsylvania and JSOU Associate Fellow*

191

Richard H. Shultz, Jr.Ph.D., Political Science*Director, International Security Studies Program, The Fletcher School and JSOU Senior Fellow*

Stephen SloanPh.D., Comparative Politics*University of Central Florida*

Robert G. Spulak, Jr.Ph.D., Physics/Nuclear Engineering*Sandia National Laboratories and JSOU Associate Fellow*

Joseph S. StringhamBrigadier General, U.S. Army, Ret.*Alutiiq, LLC and JSOU Associate Fellow*

J. Paul de B. TaillonPh.D., International Affairs*Royal Military College of Canada and JSOU Associate Fellow*

Graham H. Turbiville, Jr.Ph.D., History, *Courage Services, Inc. and JSOU Senior Fellow*

Jessica Glicken TurnleyPh.D., Cultural Anthropology/Southeast Asian Studies, *Galisteo Consulting Group and JSOU Senior Fellow*

Rich YargerPh.D., History, *Professor of National Security Policy, U.S. Army War College and JSOU Associate Fellow*

www.ingramcontent.com/pod-product-compliance
Lightning Source LLC
Chambersburg PA
CBHW060253290526
45789CB00001B/308